The People Paul Admired

The House of Prisca and Aquila

OUR MISSION AT THE HOUSE OF PRISCA AND AQUILA IS TO PRODUCE QUALITY books that expound accurately the word of God to empower women and men to minister together in a multicultural church. Our writers have a positive view of the Bible as God's revelation that affects both thoughts and words, so it is plenary, historically accurate, and consistent in itself; fully reliable; and authoritative as God's revelation. Because God is true, God's revelation is true, inclusive to men and women and speaking to a multicultural church, wherein all the diversity of the church is represented within the parameters of egalitarianism and inerrancy.

The word of God is what we are expounding, thereby empowering women and men to minister together in all levels of the church and home. The reason we say women and men together is because that is the model of Prisca and Aquila, ministering together to another member of the church—Apollos: "Having heard Apollos, Priscilla and Aquila took him aside and more accurately expounded to him the Way of God" (Acts 18:26). True exposition, like true religion, is by no means boring—it is fascinating. Books that reveal and expound God's true nature "burn within us" as they elucidate the Scripture and apply it to our lives.

This was the experience of the disciples who heard Jesus on the road to Emmaus: "Were not our hearts burning while Jesus was talking to us on the road, while he was opening the scriptures to us?" (Luke 24:32). We are hoping to create the classics of tomorrow: significant and accessible trade and academic books that "burn within us."

Our "house" is like the home to which Prisca and Aquila no doubt brought Apollos as they took him aside. It is like the home in Emmaus where Jesus stopped to break bread and reveal his presence. It is like the house built on the rock of obedience to Jesus (Matt 7:24). Our "house," as a euphemism for our publishing team, is a home where truth is shared and Jesus' Spirit breaks bread with us, nourishing all of us with his bounty of truth.

We are delighted to work together with Wipf and Stock in this series and welcome submissions on a wide variety of topics from an egalitarian inerrantist global perspective. The House of Prisca and Aquila is also a ministry center affiliated with the International Council of Community Churches.

For more information visit www.houseofpriscaandaquila.com

The People Paul Admired

The House Church Leaders of the New Testament

BEULAH WOOD

WIPF & STOCK · Eugene, Oregon

THE PEOPLE PAUL ADMIRED
The House Church Leaders of the New Testament

Copyright © 2011 Beulah Wood. All rights reserved. Except for brief quotations in critical publications or reviews, no part of this book may be reproduced in any manner without prior written permission from the publisher. Write: Permissions, Wipf and Stock Publishers, 199 W. 8th Ave., Suite 3, Eugene, OR 97401.

Scripture taken from the Holy Bible, Today's New International Version™ TNIV®. Copyright © 2001, 2005 by International Bible Society®. All rights reserved worldwide.

Wipf & Stock
An Imprint of Wipf and Stock Publishers
199 W. 8th Ave., Suite 3
Eugene, OR 97401

www.wipfandstock.com

ISBN 13: 978-1-60899-969-9

Manufactured in the U.S.A.

For a complete list of titles in the House of Prisca and Aquila Series please visit WipfandStock.com or HouseofPriscaandAquila.com

I dedicate this book to the memory of my parents, John and Ruth Baldwin, who joined others to start a house church in 1933. May these chapters strengthen many more hosts and hostesses of churches.

Contents

Preface / ix
Acknowledgments / xi

1. Hostess Mary in Jerusalem
   Promoting Prayer in Frightening Times / 1
2. Hosts Cornelius and Philip in Caesarea
   Building Hospitality and Prophetic Word / 9
3. The Leadership Team in Antioch
   No Division in Spite of Disagreement / 18
4. Hostess Nympha in Laodicea
   Gathering Household and Neighbours / 30
5. Upper-Class Philemon and Apphia in Colossae
   The New View of Social Class / 41
6. Large-Hearted Lydia and the Roman Jailer in Philippi
   Living Generously, Giving Generously / 51
7. Jason Takes Responsibility in Thessalonica
   Relationships that Reach Out / 61
8. Noble Leaders in Berea
   Sopater and Friends Search the Scriptures / 69
9. Seven Household Hosts in Corinth
   Growing the City Church Scene / 79
10. Minister Phoebe in Cenchrea
    The Protector of Many / 90
11. The Couple Ministry of Priscilla and Aquila in Ephesus
    Quintessential House Church Leaders / 101

Contents

12 Paul Teaches in Rome
    Welcome to a Rented House / 110

Bibliography / 121

Preface

THE BOOK OF ACTS and the epistles are thumbnail sketches. We easily fail to visualize behind them the lives or scenes of potential role models whose stories are told in the Scriptures. In this book, we examine geography, culture, social history, and archaeology, as well as the brief New Testament reports, to find more about the lives of householder church leaders. We look behind the scenes and reconstruct a possible context in order to form pictures in our minds. In lay terms, we will use right-brain listening and looking as well as left-brain church practice and history. We will allow narrative flow with few biblical references, for studious readers will readily find these with a concordance or electronic search. We aim to avoid the trap of theology floating separate from the reality of people in society.

An active school of ministry teaches us to use narrative to help listeners and readers see Bible characters as real people facing questions in marketplaces and meeting places, on highways and at hearths. Such first-person narratives supplement Bible study with God-given imagination, supplying details of scenes, taking listeners or readers there to ask, "What did this person feel, say, or do?" We suspend our scientific mind to hear from our relational mind. We cross over to ask, claiming possibility, not fact, "What would it be like if I were one of those people?"

Teacher of preaching Haddon Robinson says, "I am convinced that you don't really interpret the Bible unless you also use your imagination, especially with narrative literature. You have got to enter into that, not by cold analysis, but you have got to say: can I put myself back into those days, can I relive what David was feeling when he escaped from Saul? If I can do that, then I can tell the story in a vivid way."[1]

1. Duduit, "Expository Preaching in a Narrative World," 4.

Preface

Selecting leaders and cities for these chapters depended on whether the New Testament mentioned a house, a household, a church fellowship, a resident leader, or several leaders. May we all feel inspired by the lives and courage of these New Testament house church leaders, both the little-known and the well known. The Apostle Paul spoke highly of them.

Beulah Wood
Bangalore, India, and Auckland, New Zealand
March 2011

Acknowledgments

I OWE PARTICULAR GRATITUDE to Bill Spencer of the House of Prisca and Aquila for his detailed editing, and to two theological institutions: Gordon-Conwell Theological Seminary in Massachusetts, where I received encouragement to take listeners/readers to the scene, and the South Asia Institute of Advanced Christian Studies, Bangalore, south India, which gave me the opportunity to teach from the scenes of the New Testament.

1

Hostess Mary in Jerusalem

Promoting Prayer in Frightening Times

MAIN SCRIPTURE SOURCE: Acts 12:1–17

*M*ARY, MOTHER OF JOHN *Mark, had pulling power that attracted Christ-believers to her home even when it was so dangerous that the believers perhaps should not have ventured on the street. If her house lay among those of the old Jerusalem priestly families, it stood north of the western gate of the famous city. Jerusalem's topography and its people lived out their destiny as a crossroads. Physically on a 2,250-foot-high ridge, the city lay at the high point of the road that climbed from the sea thirty-three miles to the west and passed east down the hillsides that tumbled rapidly fourteen miles to Jericho and the Jordan River. Culturally, it served as a meeting ground for Jews and Arabs, traders and shopkeepers, homebodies and nonresident Jews, priests and people. Let us imagine the maid Rhoda telling what happened one April night during the Festival of Unleavened Bread a few years after the death and rising of Christ.*

One cool evening after a scorching afternoon, I looked out onto our narrow stone lane with the grimy granite underfoot between the houses. On either side stood the prettier golden granite walls of two-floored houses, with their stones joined by mud plaster. They stand upright by the sheer breadth of the walls, with windows shaped between the stones and barred with wood. We expected visitors after dark that night, but I knew they would need to take care—the path interrupted itself with occasional steps since wheels never came that way. Besides, a mule train passed through that morning, forty beasts belonging to a merchant who bought pottery and wool in the market. Our visitors would carry a light and dodge the droppings to keep their sandals clean.

I glanced past our lane to the cottage-industry crafters' shops—such a number in this city. Some supplied the building industry: masons, carpenters, plasterers. Some were part of the active textile industry: dyers, spinners, weavers, tailors, embroiderers. Some provided for personal needs or other industries: confectioners, perfumers, goldsmiths, leatherworkers, potters, rope makers, and shoemakers. But I had a lingering question: Can we trust them? Is it safe for the Christ-believing brothers and sisters to put their heads out of doors and walk these streets? Only this week, the authorities put James the brother of John to death with the sword and threw Peter in prison. We live with fear here, but we know the believers in Jesus want to come to pray. They will take the risk and come anyway.

Mary and John Mark, whom most simply call Mark, saw me as part of the family more than a servant and let me manage the door. Now, the responsibility lay with me to decide who should enter for the prayer gathering. I felt pleased that I knew the visitors from previous occasions. The first two gave a polite cough at the gate. "Come in, come in," I called. "I'm so glad you found the place in the dark."

"I wonder how many will come tonight," Mary joined in, coming to the gate. "Were you afraid on the street, knowing what they did to James on Monday?"

"Yes, we felt afraid, but we determined to come," Hoshea and Judith responded. "What if King Herod does the same to Peter as he did to James? We know we have to pray, and that your house is where the prayer meeting will be."

Inside the city wall, with sentries at the gates, we usually felt some safety from bandits, but now we all feared Herod and those who spurred him on: the Sadducees, the merchants, and the landowners. They are few in number, but they have power and wealth and do not want community disturbances to disrupt their income. Economically, they are poles apart from the ordinary small shopkeepers, peasant farmers, and craft workers. The priests try to teach the wealthy to give voluntarily to the poor, but many still struggle to live.

Hostess Mary in Jerusalem

Hoshea and Judith slipped through the gate, and I shut it quickly while they untied their shoes and left them in the courtyard.

"Here is water to wash your hands and feet," I offered. "Mark is upstairs putting out the mats for everyone."

Even water is in question in this city with only three limited sources: the pool of Siloam, the spring of Gihon, and the aqueduct the Romans built. They hardly supply normal residents, but this was Passover week. Rich or poor, every Jewish male contributes half a shekel every year to the Jerusalem temple, and from among many thousands of Jews scattered across the Roman Empire, many come for Passover. They swell the city's usual 25,000 people to 80,000, crowding all the inns. They cram the temple area, line up at all the shops that sell vegetables and lamb, and drain the water supply.

While Judith dipped water from the clay jar, she asked, "Mary, who carries the water pots to fill these large jars? It must take a long time."

"Yes it does. We all work at it: Mark, Rhoda, and I. Carrying loads like this keeps us fit," she laughed.

That is one of the fine things about working for Mary and Mark. We do the work together. We carry water, cook, or work with wool. Woolen textiles are the largest industry in the city, and we are part of that. We use three downstairs rooms to live, sleep, and eat on floor-rugs or sofas, and visitors will notice carded wool and a spinning wheel in the courtyard and a weaving loom in a side room. I spend hours spinning, and Mary weaves. Mark is usually out twelve hours a day doing his work as an apprentice.

I crossed to the raised kitchen platform in the courtyard with its earthenware cooking pots and bowls and collected small handless bowls to serve drinks of water. I carried a tray up the outside stone stairs to the large room, where I had already lit the flickering wicks of the clay lamps with their tiny pools of olive oil. I helped people take off their outside wraps and sit on the reed mats. Mary brought honey cakes, and we smiled to each as we served snacks. I ran down several times to guests at the door. Mark lifted the seal from a long cylinder to take out a parchment, for he would later read a passage from the law. One visitor asked Mary whether she ever met Jesus, so she told about herself.

"Yes, while my husband Mark was alive, we listened to Jesus' teaching and learned about the Way. We were shocked when our chief priests had Jesus executed, but, of course, everybody knows now this was not the end of the story, and that he rose again. We were with about 120 others when the Holy Spirit came, and that began the Jesus-teaching by the apostles in synagogues in Jerusalem. Then, as people offered their houses for teaching places, we invited them to ours and a group came regularly.

"Since Mark senior died, it is a great deal of work having the gatherings, but I keep welcoming everybody, because I know from the depths of my heart that Jesus is the Messiah, and I want others to know, to pray, and to receive teaching. Friends see my home as a meeting place. They know Mark, Rhoda, and I will welcome them at any time, men and women."

Judith added a comment here: "Some of the Rabbis taught that a woman should not go out in the streets, but some women always did. Rules like that are impractical when one needs water and firewood or charcoal, and, anyway, women always went to the temple to the court of the women."

"In the last few years, everything has changed about what we do," Mary continued. "Jesus talked with women, healed them, and touched them. That was unheard of before for a teacher. Women even sat with him and the disciples and talked theology. That has given me confidence about these meetings."

As a maid in her house, I have learned to respect Mary a great deal. Everybody admires her. She organizes this household and is the patron of other people who come as well. I love working in such a home, and here I came to believe in Jesus. I received practical teaching here, too, that affects even the way we receive visitors—like tonight. James, the brother of Jesus, is one of the biggest leaders in the new Messiah-believing gatherings in Jerusalem. He insists on respect and equality for all of us, though he finds some people slow to change. He grew up along with Jesus in a simple Galilee family with few privileges other than education, but his background, along with the teaching of Jesus, convinced him that followers of the Way must stop seeing people in social layers according to money or position. James scorns special treatment for rich merchants and big landowners and exposes ill-treatment of workers. Let me tell you what he taught.

James said, "Imagine a new person arrives at the house for a meeting. You notice his fine bordered robe, his gold ring, and his beautifully crafted leather money pouch, and rush to greet him enthusiastically, give him a carved chair, and wait on his needs. Then, another new person trudges in with his clothes smudged from his day's work, and you say, 'Stand there,' while you attend to the rich man and leave the new man waiting unwelcomed. Then you point in an offhand way, 'Here's a place on the mat. You can sit by my chair.'"

That pricked some of the believers' hearts! James had obviously seen a few things in gatherings and knew what sometimes happened. So, he explained, "God has chosen the weak people whom others look down on to be rich in faith and inherit the kingdom of God. Don't dishonor the poor." Then, he reminded us of Jesus' teaching: "Love your neighbor as yourself." Some find it hard to accept something else James said, though. He said, "Believers in humble circumstances ought to take pride in their high position. But the rich should take pride in their humiliation." Rich people felt uncomfortable with this, because it sounds like being a servant.

Mary and Mark, however, decided we would ignore the old social customs and be like one family of brothers and sisters, not treating me as a servant. We kept that in mind as we served the visitors who scuttled out of the dark into our house that worrisome night. Let me describe them. Hoshea was a jeweler. Judith wore a hair ornament called a "golden Jerusalem" and a gold chain around her neck, and Hoshea sported two large signet rings and a handsome cloak with a purple border. Mindful of James's teaching, Mary made no fuss over these two and guided them to sit on the reed mats beside a group of men with weather-beaten faces who had tramped in from the hills with their clothes still dusty. One was a ploughman I knew, and the others were shepherds who brought wool to the market and stopped in the city for the night. They all wore white undyed homespun, for they are ordinary people like me. The priest and his wife farther around the circle were in white, too, but with colored borders on their robes. Their gowns were linen from Galilee rather than the Jerusalem wool, for priests must wear linen.

They all took turns drinking from the earthenware bowls that Mark rinsed and brought back for the next group to use. Ploughmen and shepherds drinking from the same vessels as ordained priests is something new here, too.

Some young men farther around were fowlers with their catapults tucked into their rope belts. They sat near Hanani, an elderly potter with smudges of potter's clay on his robe, for he came straight from the potters' quarter. Then, a group of women sat and chatted. Certainly not as wealthy as the elegant wives of the priest and the jeweler, these women with the broad hands of manual labor have spent their lives milking the family cow, grinding grain, and hoeing the family garden to grow chickpeas and lentils. Next to them sat a perfume and incense merchant who sells to the temple and trades all around the Mediterranean. A small alabaster jar hung at his waist. Of course, he is visibly wealthy, but he happily sat next to the last man, a tanner with his big leather-working needle on a cord around his neck. Tradition has little good to say of tanners. Mary knew that, but she welcomed him and helped others to welcome him. You can see how transforming the teaching of Jesus and James has been in our meeting.

The prayer started. Soon, a woman with little education prayed a wandering prayer with the facts a little mixed. Nobody minded. Her prayer was important, for we were all so worried about Peter. He had come for Passover, but the rumor went around the market and temple area that he would bring Gentiles into the holy temple. King Herod arrested him and threw him into prison in the Fortress of Antonia with sixteen guards. We heard the king planned to hold a public trial the next day when festival fervor rose to a height. We saw no hope for Peter in the public square. They would probably stone him then and there.

Everybody knew the chief priests and Sadducees were extremely anxious about us Messiah-believing people. They wanted tight rules and no changes. Besides, they would never believe a crucified person could be the Messiah. In the middle of this fear, Mary was bold to hold a meeting in her house, but we *had* to pray. We begged God to protect Peter, shackled hand and foot in the fortress nearby, but we were not sure whether or not to hope. God did not rescue James, the brother of John, earlier in the week. These brothers from Galilee were part of us here in Jerusalem, and we felt churned up inside and terrified for our own lives as well.

It was late and dark when another knock sounded. I hurried down, wondering if it was too late to expect that a newcomer at that stage would be a friend. With my hand on the latch, I listened. It was Peter's voice, without a question. I raced back upstairs shouting, "Peter is standing at the door!"

"You're crazy," some twitted.

"It must be his angel," suggested others. The newcomer hovered outside knocking, still in danger. Finally, two or three men scrambled down with me and nearly fell out the door in shock. It *was* Peter. We all brought him upstairs and everyone talked at once. We laughed and retold how we could not believe it was him. Then, Peter waved his hand for us to be quiet and explained how an angel let him out of jail.

Hostess Mary in Jerusalem

"I am totally amazed," he declared. "Now I know without a doubt that the Lord sent his angel and rescued me from Herod's clutches and from everything the people were hoping would happen."

We all regained our senses a little at that point and asked, "What happens next? Will the guards arrive searching for you, Peter?"

"I'll hurry away," Peter responded. "It's too obvious for me to stay here. That would endanger all of you. I won't even tell you where I'm going. Then, if anyone tries to force you to tell where I am, you won't know anyway. Please tell James and the other brothers and sisters that I'm out of prison and safe." He left hastily.

We were astonished! So much excitement in the middle of the night! We recounted the incident again and again. "So late . . . too dangerous out in the streets . . . and we were just going to throw our cloaks over us and rest until the dawn. . . ."

"Sammy, you said 'You're crazy!' to Rhoda, though probably several of us were thinking it," someone said.

"I admit it. I'm so sorry, Rhoda. You were right after all." (I felt so included with that comment.)

"We were all part of it," added Judith. "We were so thoughtless, leaving poor Peter standing out on the street in danger, hammering at the gate."

One brother, Hanani, voiced the thoughts of many: "Mary, you achieved a fine and godly task this evening. You were courageous to welcome us in your home, and now we have seen an extraordinary answer. I wonder, friends, would the Lord have sent the angel to free Peter from the handcuffs, stocks, and prison walls if we had neglected to pray?"

"I don't know, Hanani," Hoshea replied. "But it would have been so sad for Peter, excited with a visit from an angel and escaping from the prison, if he came here and Mary, Mark, and Rhoda had gone to bed and nobody was even praying for him. Mary, we are doubly grateful for your hospitality, tonight and every other time we come."

"I agree," added Benjamin, one of the young fowlers. "Mary, something special comes from meeting in your home. You welcome us at any time of the day or night, and that is so much friendlier than it ever was going to the temple."

"Yes, Mary and Mark, we're grateful too," the priest and his wife chimed in. "A place like this is ideal. Who knows about us? Perhaps a few, but they need not know when we meet."

THE PEOPLE PAUL ADMIRED

I thought again about my beloved mistress, Mary. So brave, so kind to me and everyone else, so welcoming. Perhaps God wants us Messiah-believers to meet in homes with this richly warm hospitality. The next speaker echoed my thoughts.

"I heartily agree," Judith exclaimed. "Mary, Mark, and Rhoda are amazingly bold to encourage us to meet here, this week of all weeks, with all the turmoil and suspicion in the air. But, even in an ordinary week, they work so hard for us, bringing water, trimming and lighting all the lamps, cooking honey cakes, and especially their smiles and welcome as we come from the tension of the street to the kindness of their home. Thank you so much." They all added thanks, but Mary wanted to respond, too.

"Thank you for your kind words, everyone. We love having you all come. You know that. You know Mark and I and Rhoda want to encourage people to pray and help people to know the Messiah. That thrills us. But tonight is one of the biggest thrills in all my life. I am so happy that God answered in a spectacular way the prayers prayed under my roof. He gave us the visible proof right here. Praise him!"

She was right, of course. Whether silently or aloud, we all said, "Praise God."

READER REFLECTION

When you finish reading the chapter on Mary mother of John Mark, pause to write a list of character traits you admire in Mary. What did you learn?

SPEAKER/LISTENER EXPLORATION

If you used the chapter on Mary mother of John Mark to speak to a group, ask them to help write a list on a board of characteristics they admire in Mary. What can they take away for themselves from these thoughts?

2

Hosts Cornelius and Philip in Caesarea

Building Hospitality and Prophetic Word

MAIN SCRIPTURE SOURCES: Acts 8:4–40, 10:1—11:18, 21:8–15

CAESAREA, ALSO CALLED CAESAREA *Sebaste or Caesarea Maritime, was a leading port on the Mediterranean coast of ancestral Israel, sixty miles northwest of Jerusalem. (It had extra names to avoid confusion with Caesarea Philippi in the north of Galilee.) Paul passed through it often and knew Philip's house church and, one would expect, that of Cornelius as well. He would be an ideal person to tell us about the church leaders there. Perhaps Paul's description of the city and biography of the two leaders would go like this.*

Let me see, how many times have I passed through Caesarea now? I am in prison here, so I have plenty of time to tell you about it. It is the natural route from the coast up the hill to Jerusalem, so I have passed through often, usually boarding or leaving a ship.

Some time after I encountered Jesus on the Damascus road, Jews tried to kill me in Jerusalem, so the brothers accompanied me here on the way to Tarsus. Then, at the end of my second missionary journey, I landed at Caesarea, greeted the church here, and then traveled far north to Antioch. Another time, after about twenty years of traveling and teaching, we reached land at Tyre in Phoenicia and sailed south to Caesarea. On that visit, I stayed in the home of my good friend Philip, who has done such a great task leading a church here. Now I am here again. That is at least four times. Coming here as a prisoner was one of my misadventures! When forty men vowed to have me killed, my nephew found out, and the plot was foiled because the Jerusalem commander provided a whole platoon of guards for the journey here. For more than a year now, since I appealed to Rome, I have been detained in Caesarea under guard near King Herod's palace. They treat me well enough, and Christian leaders can visit me, but my movements are restricted since I am chained directly to my guard each day. But each of these has heard the good news of Jesus.

This is a handsome city and the capital from which Roman procurators such as Pontius Pilate govern Jerusalem and Judea under the aegis of the governor of Syria. From my slit-in-the-stones window in the barracks, I can look out across the hippodrome to the dancing glint of coastal water and, to the left, the huge columns of the palace jutting out to sea. I was taken to the palace court for hearings to give my defense in front of Felix. Later, I faced Porcius Festus there, and he invited King Herod Agrippa II and his wife Bernice along with a number of officials. The mosaic floors and tall colonnades show the wealth of the empire and the art and architecture of its artisans.

Herod the Great tried to gain favor by naming the city Caesarea for Caesar Augustus. He laid out streets as a checkerboard, with the main north-to-south street paved with limestone, and people walk among magnificent Greek-style palaces and lavish public buildings. On the shore at the southern end, a theater dedicated to the emperor Tiberius can seat four thousand people, and the hippodrome for chariot racing is 90 meters wide and 450 meters long.

Technology is a feature of this city. There is a sewer system flushed by the action of the sea, and Herod had two aqueducts built. The high-level one brings water from Mount Carmel six miles away, and the low-level one connects with the River Zarqa three miles away. Then, he developed a massive harbor by using the invention of concrete from cement made of lime and gypsum that sets under water. The artificial breakwater protecting the ships makes it the most important harbor in the region, with warehouses for trade with North Africa, Phoenicia, Spain, Italy, Greece, and Asia.

Herod provided land here to settle six thousand colonists, including soldiers, so the city has a majority of Gentiles. Not long ago, Gentiles in Caesarea treated Herod as a god, until an angel struck him and he died.

Hosts Cornelius and Philip in Caesarea

Religion here is mixed. Officially, they worship the emperor and the goddess Roma. I have seen the huge platform at the harbor edge, near the palace, where stands a temple to Augustus Caesar and Roma. However, people still worship the traditional deities like Thyche, goddess of fate or fortune, and Demeter, goddess of fruits and harvest. Jews here are a large and vocal minority with their symbol of a seven-branched candelabra, synagogues, and fiercely monotheistic traditions that reject both traditional religions and emperor worship. Tensions often mount, and things can be volatile. Added to that mix are our Jesus-believing house fellowships and their leaders, whom I want to tell about.

PHILIP THE EVANGELIST

Jewish but with Greek sympathies, Philip was a deacon serving widows when his life turned upside-down because of the persecution in which I took part in Jerusalem years ago. All credit to him, he realized the gospel message held good for all, not just Jews. He hiked north to a city in Samaria where he told people about Christ and did several miracles, especially healing paralyzed people and casting out demons. People flocked to hear him and listened intently. As a result, the city was full of joy. What a commendation! I see him as a model we can look up to—with the Holy Spirit's help, to fill a city with joy.

One conversion was remarkable. A man named Simon, a proud sorcerer who called himself The Great Power, heard Philip, believed in Jesus as the Messiah, and took baptism along with others. He had to learn a hard lesson, though. Astounded at the miracles Peter and John did, he offered money to possess the same gifts. Peter roundly rebuked him and demanded he repent, and he did.

Peter and John had arrived to check out the happenings, surprised that half-Jewish Samaritans believed in Jesus as Savior. Philip had stepped ahead of Peter and John in his practice and theology, first in preaching Jesus as Messiah to Samaritans, and then in baptizing them. But Peter and John accepted Philip's actions, taught about the Holy Spirit, and placed their hands on people to receive the Spirit. This convinced them, for some Samaritans visibly received the Holy Spirit as much as any of the believers in Jerusalem did.

Following Philip's lead, Peter and John preached the gospel in more Samaritan villages themselves. Philip had triggered a completely new approach, a change so vast that it took years for everybody to take in what a difference it would make. He simply visited where people needed to hear about Jesus and told the good news, even when he stepped outside the practice of the apostles and leaders and the church at that time. They had assumed, as so many others did, that the good news of the gospel belonged only to their own kind of people. Philip saw it was for non-Jews as well. We recognize him for that now. I think of that as my first story about Philip's leadership.

Next, Philip traveled south through the desert and fell into conversation with an even more ritually unacceptable man, a eunuch, whom Jewish law would automatically exclude because of the social rulings in the book of Deuteronomy. He was an Ethiopian court treasury official responsible to the queen of his country. Philip, forward thinker that he was, had already honored the needs of widows in Jerusalem and respected the faith of Samaritans outside Jerusalem. Now, he valued an African whom his own people would call ritually blemished.

Philip listened to this man. He did not simply announce the gospel. He dialogued, heard questions, and then led him to trust in Jesus as Savior. Then, Philip did something even more startling for a Jew. He baptized the man as a sign that he was included in the family of God and was favorably received. That was astounding at that time. What an open mind he had!

Why did he do it? Philip repeatedly listened attentively to God, another thing we admire about him. An angel told him to go to the desert road to Gaza, the Spirit told him to go to the Ethiopian's chariot and stay near, and the Spirit took Philip away suddenly. Philip allowed God's Spirit to lead and point him to the next step.

He found himself in Azotus in the Gaza area, so again told of Jesus in towns round about until he reached Caesarea, which is where I met him years later, stayed in his home, and met his family, including his four intelligent daughters. He had a thriving home fellowship going, kept in touch with believers in Jerusalem, valued prophecy, and generously offered overnight hospitality. When I left his home, a group of believers accompanied me all the way up to Jerusalem.

No wonder they call him the evangelist. Philip had a heart for reaching out to other people groups with the gospel before most others had even thought of it. What an innovator. What an unflagging friend to all. What a leader!

Hosts Cornelius and Philip in Caesarea

CORNELIUS THE HOUSEHOLDER

A Roman military man in the Italian regiment, Cornelius is the other significant Christian householder in Caesarea, and his story surprised everyone, too. He and his family honored and prayed to our Jewish God and gave gifts to needy people they knew. Yet, he had an urge to know more. God gave him a prophetic vision to send for Peter and prepared Peter with a threefold dream about clean and unclean food to make him understand that he could teach Gentiles about Christ.

As an ordinary resident of Capernaum, Peter was not as rigid as I had been as a Pharisee about keeping a large number of rules. He was prepared to stay in the home of Simon, a tanner, even though everyone knew tanners were unclean much of the time because they handled the corpses of animals. Perhaps Simon felt pleased by the welcome now open to him when followers of Christ rejected the purity laws that had kept him out. All the same, while Peter stayed with the tanner, he was surrounded by the foul smells, the vats of dark liquids, and the curing hides of the tanner's trade. Perhaps that made Peter dwell on the idea of purity, and that prepared him for his threefold vision of clean and unclean animals. Because of the vision, when Cornelius sent his devout servant and two footmen to Peter in Joppa, Peter traveled with them to Caesarea and led Cornelius to faith in Christ. Think about that. Peter needed his vision three times. Cornelius acted immediately on the one vision he received. He must have lived and prayed in a way that was sincerely open to the Almighty.

God had a plan for Cornelius. He was an acknowledged leader already, in charge of a hundred soldiers in a well-known regiment, and leading his household with wisdom and consideration. His staff thought highly of him and happily described him to Peter as "a righteous and God-fearing man . . . respected by all the Jewish people." That is worth noting. Jews knew and appreciated him, though we Jews seldom mix with Gentiles. He had dealt honestly with them and been among them enough to contribute justice and receive respect. He held a special connection with his subordinates, too—so open that, when he wanted to send to Joppa for Peter, he told his aide-de-camp and two servants all about his personal business with a vision, a voice from God, and an invitation to a man he had never seen.

THE PEOPLE PAUL ADMIRED

The scene when Cornelius's messengers returned bringing Peter also points to the high regard people held for him. Not everyone could draw a large gathering of friends and relatives to anticipate the arrival of a man they had never heard of, based on the whim of a midafternoon vision. The household and visitors had not even heard up to then whether the messengers had found Peter nor whether he was willing to travel the twenty-five miles, walking for one and a half days or riding horseback, to accept the invitation. When he would arrive would be only a guess, yet Cornelius waited with relatives, friends, and household staff, even though he did not yet have the gift of the Holy Spirit. That is a man of faith and a man to esteem!

Cornelius was already doing everything he could to serve the Creator God. The angel who brought him the message to send for Peter told him God was so pleased that his prayers and gifts to the poor had "come up as a memorial offering before God." What honorable mention. God saw his efforts as a sacrifice so good it even smelled good. I believe his heart was right before God and before people, as far as he could go with the knowledge he had.

So, then, Cornelius welcomed God's intervention in his life, and his family and acquaintances looked to him to take the lead. When he was willing to take the gigantic step of opening up to the Holy Spirit, his honest spiritual influence reached deep into their lives, too. Look what happened: The Holy Spirit came on all who heard the message. That certainly startled the conservative Jewish believers who came along with Peter. In a tangible way, with speaking tongues and praises from the mouths of Gentiles, those Jewish men could see how the Holy Spirit came on all Cornelius's non-Jewish household and friends. Cornelius continued stepping out in faith. He had led his people to baptism in the Holy Spirit; now he led them to baptism in water. Shortly, he also offered accommodation and food to Peter and his friends. That is another thing that was similar to Philip—his hospitality.

Because of Cornelius, Peter learned that God has no favorites now, but accepts all races of people who fear him and do what is right. A little later, when Peter visited Jerusalem, conservative Jewish believers accused him of going to the home of uncircumcised men and eating with them. He took up the cause and argued that non-Jews could accept the gospel and become followers of Jesus, because of what he had learned in the home of

Cornelius. (It turned out rather a false start, though. Peter, like many of us, took a long while to realize all that this would mean in practice.)

For a man like Cornelius with such organizing skills, it would be the most natural next move to start prayer, teaching, and worship in his home. He had started it already by inviting Peter, inviting a room full of people to hear him, and taking a lead in accepting faith in Jesus Christ. These folk could become the core of a new church of people who already knew him as a leader.

CHURCHES WITH PROPHETIC VISION

With the energy, faith, and gifts of Philip and Cornelius, the churches in Caesarea had a great start. Philip and Cornelius initiated them with a significant prophetic vision that came out of our older Judaism. In the past, humans did not choose prophets, and certainly not by genealogy like priests. God chose prophets, and the people recognized them because of their prophetic gifts. That is what happened here, too. Like earlier prophets, these had to be in touch with God to hear what to say about a situation, understand, live the life, and tell it around. Cornelius did that, and so do Philip's daughters.

Peter realized in prophetic preaching that Pentecost fulfilled one of the hopes of Israel: "I will pour out my Spirit on all people. Your sons and daughters will prophesy, your old men will dream dreams, your young men will see visions." This happened in truth in Caesarea. In some cities, I advise women to prophesy with their head covered so as not to offend the surrounding people, but I urge all believers to prophesy: "Follow the way of love and eagerly desire spiritual gifts, especially the gift of prophecy. . . . Those who prophesy speak to people for their strengthening, encouragement, and comfort."

The work of Philip and then Cornelius and his household also placed high value on baptism, which proved vital as more churches developed. They set the pattern. Baptism was not new; it was in the ritual when an immigrant among us became a Jew. In the teaching of Jesus, water signified cleansing, and baptism, when a person was saturated with water, marked clearly the start of living a different life. The Ethiopian court official expected the symbol of baptism even before Philip mentioned it.

There is another point here. Philip, Peter, and then Cornelius gave baptism a meaning beyond that in Judaism. They used it for those being baptized to confess their belief in Christ and submit to his authority, and then said they baptized in the name of Jesus Christ. Philip did this with the Samaritans and Peter with Cornelius. Baptism also pointed to receiving the Holy Spirit. Philip observed this along with Peter and John when they laid hands on the Samaritans. Later, a few dozen people saw the effects of the Holy Spirit in Cornelius's home, so that all agreed that, since they had received the Holy Spirit, they could be baptized.

Being baptized was the way to enter the warmth and participation of our fellowships, being cleansed, promising to serve Christ, and receiving the Holy Spirit into one's life. Philip and Cornelius promoted it in their lives and in their service.

So what is the church like in Caesarea? Let me start with a question I cannot fully answer about the leaders here. If Philip was already in Caesarea, would it not have been easier for God to send Cornelius to him for teaching instead of calling Peter? This is a guess, but perhaps Peter needed to learn to reach out to people who were not like him. Philip already knew that. Given the racial composition and religious pluralism of Caesarea, for the Caesarea church to accept racial diversity would become more and more vital. The fellowships started here were among the earliest highly multicultural Christian gatherings.

The evangelistic heart of Philip, and Cornelius's desire for teaching, must have done much for the new churches. I saw them develop as I passed through, appreciating Philip's hospitality. Philip encouraged in others initiative and confidence. I saw this when the group of disciples accompanied our party to Jerusalem after we stayed with them. Philip could have claimed the right to accompany us, but he happily gave the task to other disciples, people whom he had trained. He was not claiming control for himself, but empowering others. I saw it again when he welcomed Agabus, a visitor they knew from Jerusalem, to contribute his gift of prophecy about me within their fellowship of believers.

Then, also, Philip's four unmarried daughters prophesied regularly. Some people could say it is not wise for a church leader to give the respect of being a prophet to young people, or they might say it is inappropriate to encourage one's family to prophesy publicly. But Luke, my fellow missionary, and I thought it was in order and had no criticisms. The church members accepted the four young women as prophets before I stayed in the home on that trip. Luke was impressed, for one does not often find four sisters who serve the church as prophets. These young women are integral to God's plan for the ministry here and serve God by bringing his message to their fellow believers. Their ministry says something more about Philip's integrity too—even the family members who know him best gladly follow his God. Think what a message about family life those young women can take with them. When the purpose of prophecy is to build up believers, they could do it well because of the home life Philip gave them and the gifts of the Holy Spirit.

While I am held under guard here and allowed visitors, Philip or one of his daughters or other people in the house churches visit and talk to me to give me company; they pray for me when there is a hearing; they cook and bring food. At times, several of them come to sit nearby, and I teach. It is fine if the guards hear, too. Since I have appealed to Caesar, I shall leave from here for Rome, but I am confident as I leave the believers here. Their leaders are doing a great job.

The port city of Caesarea offers a safe harbor on an inhospitable coast. Churches today, small or larger, can and must become safe harbors for those who would follow Christ in an anxious world. That is what Philip and Cornelius have done for believers in Caesarea.

READER REFLECTION

When you finish reading the chapter on Philip and Cornelius, write two headings: *Freedom to hear from God* and *Frameworks for church membership*. List under these the examples of what Philip and Cornelius contributed in Caesarea and other places. What can you learn for today's ministry?

SPEAKER/LISTENER EXPLORATION

If you used the chapter on Philip and Cornelius to speak to a group, ask them to help write on a board under two headings, *Philip* and *Cornelius*, a list of ways in which the personality of each of these leaders brought both freedom to hear from God and frameworks of church membership. What can we apply to our ministries today?

3

The Leadership Team in Antioch

No Division in Spite of Disagreement

LEADERS IN THE CHURCH: Simeon, Lucius, Manaen, Barnabas, Paul, and Peter

MISSIONARIES: Barnabas, Paul, Silas, and John Mark

MAIN SCRIPTURE SOURCES: Acts 11:19–30, 12:25—13:3, 14:26—15:41

RAPIDLY, IN THE EARLIEST days of churches, those in Jerusalem and Syrian Antioch became the two lead churches. Then, the initiative shifted even more to Antioch, probably because of the wise decision making the church and its leaders employed and because of the severe persecution in Jerusalem. Choosing Lucius, one of the five resident leaders, to tell about the church in Antioch could be a good move. Would his story go like this?

Thank you for asking me to tell about the believers in our city and how we somehow hang in together. Here, we have faced harassment and name-calling, but not the persecution and threat to life and property that some churches face. Yet, we have felt stressed almost beyond what we could bear at times because of internal disputes and clashes of personality—even between the top gospel preachers. Somehow, with God's help, we still work together. It is quite a story.

I will tell you about myself first so you have that background. Though I settled in Antioch, I am a Jew, born in Cyrene in Libya in North Africa. It is a handsome Roman city like Antioch, on a slope back from the sea,

The Leadership Team in Antioch

and our Jewish colony there has functioned for nearly six hundred years. However, I have traveled a lot. I did my training, along with others from Africa and Asia, at the Synagogue of Freedmen in Jerusalem. These synagogue Jews were so much against Christ that they led the persecution of Stephen. They roused a mob against him, claimed he had blasphemed, and incited the Sanhedrin against him. They stoned Stephen, and that set off the whole rampage of persecution that followed.

In Jerusalem, I learned of Jesus Christ and believed, but Jerusalem soon became too hot for us. Some fellow Jews from Cyrene had already drawn attention in connection with Christ. Simon was the man the Romans forced to carry the cross of Christ, and, at Pentecost, some of my friends gained mention because they understood what Peter said just as if it had been in the Cyrenaica language. The persecution was so bad that, while some stayed, many left the city and scattered farther north along the eastern side of the Great Sea-at-the-Middle-of-the-Earth to places like Tyre, Sidon, Byblos, Cyprus Island, and Antioch. My friend Simeon Niger gave me the idea to go, too.

"I'm taking my family to Syrian Antioch," he said. "This persecution in Jerusalem is frightful, but God could use it."

"How could that be?" I grumbled.

"If we go north, we'll meet more people to whom we can tell the good news."

"But why Antioch? It's three hundred miles away!"

"Yes, but, as you know, it's the capital of Syria and the third city in the empire after Rome and Alexandria. Transport hub. Trade routes east, west, north, and south. To preach there would be so influential."

"You make it look as if we're making the decisions, and not us on the defensive facing Pharisees, Sanhedrin, and temple police."

I liked Simeon's next answer. He said, "It might look as if we are on the defensive, but it is all planned by God to spread us widely with the gospel."

So, my wife and I packed our kitchen gear and some clothes and parchments in boxes, had them taken down by packhorse to Caesarea to a northbound ship, and joined the other refugee believers. Secretly, we were not just refugees, but people with a mission.

Antioch was impressive: more like the green of fertile Cyrene than the dry hills of Jerusalem. We approached through Seleucia, the river-mouth city, and spent a day riding the boat sixteen miles up the Orontes

THE PEOPLE PAUL ADMIRED

River to the Antioch docks. I have never seen such a beautiful approach to a city. The sailors paddled us between gardens and orchards on one of the busiest inland trade paths of the world. We saw ships laden with wines, silk, vegetables, and grain. Five miles from the city, we saw the steep hills of Daphne with their famous flowers and rose gardens. Perfumers make scents there for the wealthy. On the river edge were country houses, Roman-style villas, and inns stocked with farm produce and fruit juices cooled in cellars.

Farther upstream, we saw 1,500-foot-high Mount Silpius and, below it, the bustling river city. We passed its large hippodrome racecourse and saw the theater, the aqueduct for water supply, and the public baths added by Emperor Julius. Augustus Caesar set up Olympic-type games here with drama and music as well as athletic races. In recent years, Herod the Great paved the two-mile main street with marble stones to thirty-one feet wide. Emperor Tiberius lined the famous street with colonnades on each side and vaulted stone roofs on pillars at intersections using 3,200 stone columns, many of pink and grey granite, with bronze decorations to shelter the people walking to the shops and villas. We thought it was extremely handsome.

Ten miles of city walls pass around the city with its streets laid out in a tidy rectangular grid for a population of 500,000. People call the city "Queen of the East." The river does flood at times, yet the city survives and prospers with its own constitution and pays no taxes to Caesar. People say retired government officials spend fortunes here, gambling on chariot races, relaxing in the public baths, and indulging in exotic foods.

Simeon met us at the river wharf and helped us find a house. Jews are about one-seventh of the population, mostly in the Jewish quarter, Kerateion. We do not feel out of place in such a cosmopolitan city with its quarter for Greeks, a sector for native Syrians, Roman soldiers, traders, slaves, and sailors from all over the empire.

Most houses are situated along the flowing river. There is a bountiful market with fruit, vegetables, flowers, eggs, and fish. At the port, like bees around a hive, workers loaded and unloaded goods at vessels from far and near. Camels and mules stomped as they waited in line for their loads, for Antioch sends textiles, wines, copper, tin, lead, and vessels of bronze, silver, and glass to Persia and India. It imports carpets, embroidery, furs, and hides from Babylon and Persia, and pottery and ivory from India. Silk comes from China, perfumes and drugs from Arabia, and dried fish

The Leadership Team in Antioch

from Egypt. Gold, jewels, and slaves arrive from Egypt, and horses from Spain for the hippodrome races. It takes about seventy days on the caravan route from Antioch to Babylon, and even more to Rome by boat.

The wealthy love their entertainment here: theater drama, chariot races at the hippodrome, athletics at the stadium, public baths, music and dancing displays, gladiators fighting wild beasts, hunting and fowling outside the city. But tragedies affect all classes. Antioch is prone to earthquakes. Many died in a severe quake about seventy years ago, and again in another about three years ago.

Simeon took us to meet Manaen, a foster brother of Herod the Tetrarch and a believer. We wanted to tell the good news about Jesus, so we asked Manaen to fill us in on the religious scene in the city.

"Oh, it's a melting pot," he exclaimed. "A religiously plural society, yet they don't like rival religions. While Jesus walked in Judea and Galilee, Tiberius Caesar was reinforcing pagan religion here by restoring, building, and rebuilding huge temples to Jupiter, Dionysius, and Pan. A temple to Apollos draws people to the sacred groves of Daphne. People worship the goddess Tyche for prosperity and good luck. She is pictured crowned and draped in a long robe, seated on a rock with a sheaf of wheat for prosperity in her right hand, and, below her, representing the river, a youthful swimmer. To the south at Baalbek, between the Lebanon and Anti-Lebanon mountain ranges, they have started another huge temple complex with the tallest temple columns in the known world, to worship Baal and the sun. Pagan religion is full of energy and growth. Besides, people are supposed to worship the emperor in Rome, and many still worship their old family gods as well.

"So, how is it for Jews?"

"Jews are accepted in Antioch. People usually do not persecute us. They respect our ethics. And Jews from here send handsome donations to the temple in Jerusalem." I sat with Simeon and Manaen and heard how some of the Jews already believe in Jesus as the Messiah, and non-Jews, too, have believed. That was exciting and different. The three of us coached other new believers, and people enthusiastically told the good news to their workers, relatives, and acquaintances. Even more believed because the Lord's hand was with us. Most believers elsewhere only tell the good news to other Jews, but we tell it to non-Jews as well, and scores have believed.

THE PEOPLE PAUL ADMIRED

Word of this trickled back south to Jerusalem, especially the fact that so many non-Jews now believed. The leaders there were not expecting this, so they sent one of their senior leaders, Barnabas, to find out what was happening. That was a turning point, for he checked out what these new people believed and gave the work his blessing.

"I'm thrilled with what is happening here," he said. "This is God's grace. He is giving enlightenment to non-Jews and forgiving them just as much as he forgives us. I'm so glad. Just one thing I ask, though. Never turn back. Keep learning about Christ, and growing. Then none of us will feel ashamed of being people who started out on the path and then gave up."

Barnabas stayed for a while and gave teaching for everyone. People could see he was a good man and full of the Holy Spirit. They loved to learn from him, and even more people became believers, which, of course, brought more changes.

"So many people need teaching here!" he exclaimed. "I can't give all they need. I know someone to call on for help, and that's Paul. It's only a short sea voyage to Tarsus. I'll take the trip and fetch him." So, when Paul came back with Barnabas, the two taught us in Antioch for a whole year. What a treat! Gentiles were lining up to follow Christ, and new believers were learning the Christian life.

There—I have used the word *Christian*. It was invented right here in Antioch. People noticed we were not the same as other Jews and now had among us dozens of non-Jews. They coined the word *Christian* as a taunt, meant to embarrass us, but we were proud of the label. My friends were prepared to be different, and that is not easy in a religiously plural environment where looking to one God alone is scorned. Besides, worshiping the emperor was a civic duty, and worshiping local gods was honored as a part of every home. But our *Christians* were willing to take the consequences. Some lost jobs, some lost customers and trading opportunities in their businesses. Some lost closeness to family members. Discrimination hurts. My family was new here, but I could see the harassment.

Still, perhaps Antioch did Christians a favor in giving us a name. It has become a type of shorthand. The earlier labels were longer: "those who believe," "those who call on the name," "those who received the word," and "those who are being saved." Some of the letters we send to each gathering refer to people "of the way," "of the way of the Lord," "saints," or "the people of God." The word *disciple* was used, too. Nobody limited it to

The Leadership Team in Antioch

the twelve men who followed Jesus. Our fellowship of disciples included everyone who was learning, and that was all of us.

Then, although we are three hundred miles away, we had more visitors from Jerusalem: this time, some prophets. Agabus was one. One Sunday at one of our gatherings, he stood up and prophesied: "I have a specific message from God. Something bad is going to happen all over the Roman Empire—a famine. It will be serious for all of us, but especially serious in Jerusalem and Judea where our friends are already persecuted."

We all sat up and listened. Jerusalem, where many of us had lived, and where some of us still had loved family members, was the mother church in the city where Jesus died.

"What can we do?" we asked ourselves. "How can we help them?" There were five of us leaders by then: Manaen, Simeon, and me, and now Barnabas and Paul. People were saying they wanted to send a monetary gift and agreed to take up a collection to send money to help the believers in Judea. That was an experience for our fellowship, too. You should have seen how generously our folk gave. Some were business families who had resources and could easily give, but others were ordinary day-workers. To their credit, each gave as much as they could.

"How shall we send this?" we wondered.

"Barnabas has not been back to his people for some years," someone commented. "Let's send him. He came here representing the fine leaders of the Jerusalem churches. Now let's reverse it and send him as our representative to them."

"Then Paul should be the second person, so he meets the elders there," added another. So, with prayers against bandits and storms, we sent them off, each with a belt of money for the mother churches and their members back in Judea. We found out later that this was a first. We were the first to send finances to another church in a needy time.

When Paul and Barnabas returned, they brought John Mark, too, a relative of Barnabas. It was to his mother's house that Peter had hurried in the middle of the night when an angel got him out of prison. When Mark told us the story, we were all delighted.

Because Antioch sits across the trade routes, we constantly heard news of other countries, and soon our fellowship wanted to send someone to tell the good news in other cities. The five of us led the Christians in worship and fasting. When we met up again—Manaen, Simeon, and I, joined by so many members—we felt God had pointed us to sending

THE PEOPLE PAUL ADMIRED

Paul and Barnabas. From one point of view, we were reluctant to lose our most experienced leaders who had taught here for a year, but they had no hesitations. New adventures—fine; dangerous travel—nothing new! They were ready to head off for an out-of-the-way island, Cyprus, or even north to Asia Minor.

We again fasted and prayed, then commissioned them with our hands on their shoulders: "God in Heaven, we send these two brothers as our representatives and yours. They are on kingdom duty for you. Please keep them safe and make their mission hugely effective. Work in them by your Holy Spirit. Enable them to bring many into your kingdom and train them to be true disciples."

Our unity in Antioch in making significant decisions was noteworthy, considering our mixed leaders' group that included Barnabas from Jerusalem, Simeon Niger with his Latin-sounding name that means "black," myself a North African Jew, high-society Manaen, and former Pharisee Saul from Tarsus, another nonresident Jew. Alongside us were newer Syrian believers, some very different from us. Jews are people of a book. Along with our farming and primary trades, literacy is highly valued among us, and we tend toward theorizing and sometimes theoretical disputes. In contrast, this city flourishes with trading wide and far. Traders have their contacts in Crete, Alexandria, Tyre, Babylon, and Rome. And home-based industry absorbs many of our associates. They spin and weave using wool, silk, or linen. Masons split, shape, and chisel stone. Carpenters saw, chisel, and nail timber for doors, plows, or beds. Many younger men and a few women stay bonded as apprentices for up to ten years. Indeed, the contrast stood out. While the city offered abundant wealth and entertainment, Christians fasted and prayed. Where their fellow Jews and the thousands of traders and wealthy retired people were either making money or spending money, these house church leaders were denying themselves. Self-serving and competition were not part of their thinking. This was amazing.

As a result, our diverse group worked together in harmony, reaching a concerted decision. Unanimously, we agreed to send Paul and Barnabas, with their young assistant John Mark, down to the coast at Seleucia where they caught a boat to Cyprus to preach the good news. There, they traveled the whole island as evangelists and then crossed to the mainland at Perga far to the west of Paul's hometown, Tarsus. When they continued north to the other Antioch, John Mark headed back to Jerusalem. No

The Leadership Team in Antioch

doubt, he responded to the family duty of watching out for his mother's wellbeing. Paul and Barnabas experienced a whole gamut of rejection, success, stoning, healings, adulation, persecution, and joy in the Holy Spirit, and then sailed from Perga home to us at Antioch. It was as if we in Antioch were the strategists of sending to other places. The missionaries reported back to us, and the whole church backed them. Our travelers told us about their adventures and the open door of faith in Jesus through which God was leading many non-Jews as well as Jews. But herein lay the seeds of differences of opinion for us: John Mark turning back, and the welcome and equality given to non-Jews, both here and elsewhere.

It happened when Peter came from Jerusalem. At first, he willingly ate food with non-Jewish believers, but he stopped when others also arrived, including Timaiah and Elia. They were teachers, and their teaching went like this: "All you men have to be circumcised. You must obey the law of Moses. If you object to this, God will not save you."

This teaching affected individuals and families. Baltasar and his wife Yalda invited brother Timaiah to a meal at their place, and Timaiah said, "I'm terribly sorry. I can't eat with you because Baltasar is not circumcised." I knew Baltasar and Yalda felt offended by that. They thought Timaiah was treating them as if they were not good enough for his company.

Two Syrian men, Sargon and Asu, started to arrange with Timaiah and Elia to be circumcised along with their sons, but Sargon's educated wife, Sabeen, said, "Well, you can become an accepted believer, but what about me? I don't want to become a Jew in order to become a Christian. In any case, I can't be circumcised like a man. Does that mean I can't be fully accepted as a follower of Christ?"

When Paul and Barnabas heard about this unhappy talk, they were ready the next time Timaiah and Elia were teaching, and disagreed sharply with them. "We don't teach circumcision here," they said. "Please be quiet. You are out of order with this teaching. God welcomes both Jews and non-Jews and does not require them to be circumcised."

"No, you are wrong," they said. "Every male has to be circumcised if he wants to serve Jehovah God."

"Stop saying that," Paul retorted. "That is contrary to the freedom of faith we have in Christ. Will you sit down and stop giving that teaching to our gathering?"

That interchange was bad enough, but then problems arose between Paul and Peter, for Peter took the side of Timaiah and Elia. Now, we saw two highly respected leaders going at each other hammer and tongs over inter-dining.

Paul opposed Peter to his face. "Your teaching stands condemned," he claimed sternly. "You are being controlled by James back in Jerusalem. Before these others came from him, you ate food with non-Jews and did not care whether it was kosher or not. Now you hang back and cut yourself off from them, refusing to eat with them. You are a coward. You are afraid of those people who are pushing for circumcision."

"Be quiet, Paul," Timaiah and Elia retorted. "Who said you were the boss? The Antioch church is not the leading church. That has to be Jerusalem, and it is led by Brother James. We and Peter are representatives from there."

Paul became convinced that the visitors, and especially Peter, were not acting rightly in view of the real gospel and decided to have it out with Peter. In front of them all, he stood up and said, "You are a Jew, yet you live like a non-Jew. You personally have not bothered about the food laws in the last few years. You are a hypocrite. You saw that people in Samaria and Caesarea received the Holy Spirit without being circumcised. We Jewish believers know that a person does not become right before God by keeping the old Jewish law, but by faith in Jesus Christ. We have put our faith in Christ Jesus alone, not in keeping the law. You know as well as I do that keeping the law does not make anyone right before God. How come you want to force non-Jews to keep our laws that do not even work?"

Peter and the others were left stuttering at this point. Paul had not run out of steam, though. He wound up the confrontation further.

"It's like this. We Jewish believers want to be made right by Jesus Christ, but does Christ tell us to obey the Jewish laws? Absolutely not. We're trying to destroy dependence on the law. To rebuild it would make us break the law. Look at this logic. If any of us could become righteous in God's sight by keeping the law, then Christ would not have had to die. His death would be wasted."

Caught between our senior leaders by all this, Manaen, Simeon, and I were feeling tense ourselves. Their arguing was so sharp. We thought highly of the Jerusalem visitors, but our own men were against them. We headed for the background for a quiet discussion, and we came up with a suggestion.

"We need a decision on this not only for ourselves, but for all the churches. We need it talked through properly," Simeon announced. "Paul

The Leadership Team in Antioch

and Barnabas and three or four others who can be spared from their businesses, we want you to take a boat south to Jerusalem to talk to the elders and other apostles. Let them call on leaders from other churches too, from Byblos, Sidon, Tyre, and even some from Samaria—get them to go, too. This needs a formal statement after all sides are heard."

"Yes, we'll do that," Peter, Paul, Barnabas, and the other visitors from Jerusalem agreed. So, off they sailed for Jerusalem. They actually enjoyed the trip, as they had such grand news to share as they stopped by the other churches telling how many people had believed in Jesus.

I will not go into all the details of the council in Jerusalem. One good thing was that Peter, Paul, and Barnabas argued on the same side. The council listened and finally reached a policy: Christians would live free of laws about who to dine with, and nothing was said about circumcision. That modeled collaborative decision making by both our Antioch leaders and the Jerusalem leaders. The great point for us was that Paul and Barnabas came back, with representatives Judas Barsabbas and Silas, bearing a clear statement they all agreed to, saying the only requirements were to avoid idol-sacrificed food, blood and strangled meat, and sexual immorality.

We were relieved and happy, but our discussion was not quite over. We called a gathering of the church and included everyone in hearing the letter. When all had heard or read it, they were glad and encouraged. After all, carrying out the decisions would be the responsibility of the whole church, not just the leaders. The whole church had sent the deputation, and the whole church heard the report back. We believe everyone is responsible for making decisions and for carrying them out. That is collaborative church decision making.

But the content of the decision was important, too. Freedom to follow Christ is more important than cultural norms. The mother church, Jerusalem, did not impose its culture on the daughter church. The Antioch believers did not limit how they lived and worshiped to the pattern of those who brought the gospel to them, but developed their own culture of how to live as Christians.

This decision helped things settle down. The believers received the teaching of Judas Barsabbas and Silas, and, to our great comfort, Paul and Barnabas, joined by other teachers, got on with the task of teaching the believers and inquirers the word of God. The disagreement was over—or

THE PEOPLE PAUL ADMIRED

so we thought. That one was over, but later a new dispute grew between our two heroes themselves.

"Let's head off on another mission, Barnabas," Paul urged. "We could visit the believers in the towns where we preached and encourage them to keep on for God—then perhaps go farther."

"I agree," Barnabas responded. "And let's take John Mark too, like we did before. He helped us, and it was good learning for him."

"No, we won't," Paul snapped. "He let us down. I'm not taking him."

"Oh, Paul, of course he can come. Don't be so rigid."

"No, I won't have him. He deserted us. What kind of reliability is that?"

They were off again. Fiery tempers and sharp words. I know why they are leaders: such strong personalities. But, again, an argument was in danger of splitting our church. John Mark was good friends with the son of Sargon and Yalda, so they supported him. Yalda told Sabeen, "I'm so concerned for widow Mary back in Jerusalem. Imagine how she will feel with Paul treating her son Mark so badly."

Sabeen passed this on to Baltasar: "You know, we ought to support Barnabas and John Mark in this. Paul is too intolerant of the mistakes of youth."

But others had a different view. Adad said, "I have been so blessed by Paul's teaching. He can't in the wrong." Adad's brother and his wife, Ashur and Ishtar, fully agreed, saying, "Paul is the most educated of any Christians alive. He can't be wrong. Let us stick by our teacher and give him our support."

Simeon, Manaen, and I kept pouring oil on troubled waters at our house gatherings. I won't say it did not take a great deal of work. Perhaps you can start to guess how many meetings of groups and how many private conversations and how many discussions we put into keeping us all together.

The two leaders parted and left separately, but a remarkable thing happened. We won out in our task. We kept the church together. When Barnabas and Mark left by boat for Cyprus, and when Paul and Silas left through Syria, the believers came out to pray, to commend them to God's mercy, and to send them on their way. The sharp disagreement between leaders did not split the church. Our collaboration was so strong that quarreling could not divide us. Our city of Antioch continued as the prime missionary-sending church and the base for the operations of Paul,

The Leadership Team in Antioch

Barnabas, Silas, and others. And Paul and John Mark later reconciled. Praise God.

READER REFLECTION

When you finish reading the chapter on the Antioch leaders, pick out six of their positive features. Now, make a checkmark next to each feature you practice in any responsibility you have. Consider how you would wish to change what you do in light of their examples.

SPEAKER/LISTENER EXPLORATION

If you used the chapter on the Antioch leaders to speak to a group, list out the features of their leadership styles. Put a checkmark next to the features that are methods you could use in the present day.

4

Hostess Nympha in Laodicea

Gathering Household and Neighbours

MAIN SCRIPTURE SOURCE: Colossians 4:15–16, Revelation 3:14–22

*W*HAT WE KNOW OF *Nympha as a person springs primarily from two small verses written by Paul about AD 58 to 60. "Give my greetings to the brothers and sisters at Laodicea, and to Nympha and the church in her house. After this letter has been read to you, see that it is also read in the church of the Laodiceans and that you in turn read the letter from Laodicea" (Col 4:15–16).*

The quotation still leaves questions. We do not have a letter written at this stage either from or to Laodicea, though we do have John's letter to Laodicean believers in his Revelation more than twenty years later. Today, Colossae, Laodicea, and Hierapolis (then a bustling Roman spa town because of its natural hot water springs and white silica terraces) are uninhabited ruins not far from one another in a broad valley. Tourists stay at modern Pamukkale down the slope from Hierapolis, where excavations reveal the Roman town. The modern museum in Hierapolis has many exhibits from Roman times, and modern tourists have stepped barefoot across the beautiful white silica terraces. Earthquakes have damaged the terraces, too. There was an earthquake in AD 60, perhaps shortly after the mention of Nympha in the letter to Colossae.

Nympha as a householder had a large enough home for family and probably resident staff, perhaps a steward like Deniz and his wife Almas, and other workers. Almas could tell about Laodicea and the possible household workings of their patron, Nympha.

I am pleased to tell you about Laodicea, for it is a grand place with a wonderful view. Our city was founded by Antiochus II more than two hundred years ago and named after his wife Laodicea. I stand here on the flagstone slabs of the road between the houses where our town perches atop a broad spur between two streams flowing down to the wide valley when we look across to the south. To the east, seven miles away, the surprising splash of white on the dark hillside marks the white terraces of Hierapolis. Up the hill behind us to the north, ample common land and trees slope to the valley floor. The Roman road running through here and down the wide valley to Ephesus on the coast is a necessity for our small city's trade. With it, Laodicea grew prosperous, a center for commerce and trade, for the road runs from the Euphrates River far to the east, through Antioch in Pisidia, through Hierapolis, then west along the Lycus valley and the winding Meander River, to Ephesus on the coast a hundred miles away. If I shade my eyes, I see a mule train, porters straining under backloads, and a military roadwork party. We are on a crossroads where our houses and businesses group around the intersection with the road from Sardis to Perga. Our wealth funded two theaters on the northeast slope, one Greek and one Roman, and a stadium where we hold Olympic-type games.

Wealthy families here live in separate two-story stone houses with courtyards inside, but Nympha's is one of the several conjoined houses on the main street. They are built for business or trade downstairs with artisan and street-front rooms, household rooms upstairs, and more rooms farther back. We have church in a large room upstairs. Nympha's father gave this house to her as her dowry, so it never belonged to her husband. She ran her business here even before he died, and Deniz and I are her trusted retainers.

I look after the food for my mistress and her workers. In this valley, most people have enough to eat. You should see our orchards in late summer: peaches, apples, cherries, nuts, and especially figs. We dry and export figs; we have so many. With a young woman to help, I keep a garden for the household outside the town. We grow lentils, beans, chickpeas, lettuce, onions, radishes, and cucumbers. Then we intermingle spices—mustard, caraway, rue, and sage. Nympha employs a farm manager, too, as we need grains. In most households, we reckon on nearly a pound of wheat or barley per person per day through the year. That means time-consuming plowing, planting, harvesting, and winnowing. Some days are hazy, with women on the slope below throwing the wheat in the air to let the chaff blow away in the breeze. We half-grind some of the wheat for porridge, but we also need flour. Two of our maidservants work at the large grindstone. Excuse me a minute.

"How are you, Dilara? Is your mother better from that fever? And Elif, your baby is due in a month, is it? Don't take your turn at the wheel. You could hurt yourself. You just pour the grain in the hole at the top and collect the flour from the chute at the side. Don't carry water from the stream, either. Those earthen pots are heavy. Don't even carry it from the stone tap on the aqueduct from Hierapolis."

Here is the pottery oven, like a monster jar, over a fire behind the house. Every day, Dilara and Elif grind whole-grain flour for flatbread or raised bread. For a festival, we cook sheep meat or goat meat. Often, we buy charcoal from the charcoal burners who go farther afield and set up camps to burn wood. Dilara and Elif regularly bring down backloads of firewood, too.

Here is Deniz coming from checking the flock with the shepherd. Mistress Nympha has 120 sheep, nearly all black, as that is the special business of the area. Meet Hakan and his daughter Ceren. Ceren is brilliant at caring for sickly lambs and helps the shearers clip the wool before the summer. We have such a number of people in the household because there are so many tasks for us to work on and with which we support one another.

All of us spin in our spare time. Often, our shepherds stand on the hills twirling a spindle with a long, weighted wooden stem to make a ball of wool from carded fleece. There is a fuller's wool-washing trough outside, and the loom is in the lower floor of the house. We weave the wool to make and sell cloaks and other clothing. Our city's textile trading is famous for black wool, organized under a powerful business association called the Most August Guild of Wool Washers. Specialized sheep-breeding produces soft, black, glossy wool that can make plain tunics with purple borders and fine cloaks that are almost rain repellent.

Sometimes, we provide lodging for travelers, especially people who come to the city for its celebrated eye salve. Laodicea boasts a school of medicine with specialty ointments for eyes and ears. The names of two doctors are stamped on the city's coins, and patients who come for treatment can find board as paying guests in the homes along the main road.

I must tell you about Mistress Nympha. As a higher-class person, she wears a long-sleeved dark wool tunic, sandals, and a cloak across her shoulders if it is cool. She keeps her work and living room scented with a potpourri of rose petals to counter the earthy smells outside. She is wonderfully welcoming. I have heard her say, "Welcome, strangers. You are not strangers if you are Christ-followers. You are brothers and sisters."

Mistress Nympha has held church in the home here for a few years now, since Epaphras journeyed to the Lycus Valley from Ephesus and brought the gospel news to Colossae. After the church started in Philemon and Apphia's house, some from there hiked across to here, about eleven miles, and told the gospel first to the Jewish community. Epaphras has visited us, too. He knows us well and prays for the churches in our three cities. He still sends all of us greetings when he can.

Most people live in households like ours with a core family, extended family, slaves, freedmen and freedwomen, hired workers, and sometimes tenants. At times, trading partners in the wool business stay a night or two as well. In the past, people usually got on together well, since we all knew our place. Nobody tried to be an actual friend of Nympha. She made the decisions, and we all knew from whom we took orders in every detail of life. When Nympha and a few of us believed and accepted baptism, the atmosphere changed. We still know who is the leader for work areas and who is higher on the social scale, but we listen to each other more, we eat food together, and we help each other in our tasks more.

The initiative for that came from Nympha, of course. What did she do? She listened to us. She called Deniz, Hakan, and Ceren and said, "Now, tell me how the sheep are this season. How many ewes had twins? Is the wool dark and glossy?"

Hakan said, "The ewes are healthy, madam, but no twins. And some bore lambs too early, and they died in the cold weather." We talked through the questions together, and then she asked us for suggestions. Hakan added that there were more twins across the valley and suggested, "Shall I buy some ewe lambs from over there? There will be more chance of twinning."

"Yes, that seems good. Ceren, you go, too, to help bring them back."

Ceren, too, would speak. She could suggest, "Ma'am, I would not let the rams run with the flock until November. Then, the lambs will not be born until April." In discussions like this, Nympha listened to her staff. She discussed with me and Deniz the carding, the work of the fuller, the spinning, and the preparation of loads for the traders. I planned with her the vegetables and spices the workers would grow. Deniz talked over the rotation of the field crops.

Nympha told us, "I feel different about my staff these days. You are my brothers and sisters as believers. I have learned we are all made in the image of God, and so we all must respect one another and hear from one another. I want to do this with all our workers. I'm hoping you will do it for one another, too." She set such an example that we did learn to do that. We cooked for one another and often ate together.

Then, Nympha pointed us to the shared meal as Christians. "The way we remember what Jesus did for us is with Communion," she said. "During our prayer and worship in this home, we will be like brothers and sisters in sharing the bread and wine that remind us of Christ's death for us." We did that, too, and it felt special that the old social barriers had gone. "We are not brothers and sisters by birth," Nympha said, "but we are certainly that by new birth."

We heard about Brother Paul, the apostle. He was the one who sent Epaphras to our valley. Travel like that is easier now than it was years ago because of the roads the Romans built and maintain across our region, Anatolia. Paul traveled easily to Pisidian Antioch and went from place to place in Galatia and Phrygia, strengthening the believers. News travels fast with traders. We in the Lycus Valley knew that Paul was in Ephesus at the time of the riot over the goddess Artemis. There was a great deal of talk about that here. Religion is a popular subject in Anatolia. On the surface, community life revolves around worshiping the emperor in Rome, though, in fact, people also worship Greek gods and many still adhere to earlier local gods. One of their favorites is called Men Karou. Some worship and build statues for their god, like the one of Isis in the monumental fountain. They even mix older with newer gods. Still, the public calendar and daily life and trading days for a household in our small city are shaped to observe days, months, and years in honor of the Caesar.

Chief citizens aiming for social and political prestige build temples and stage festivals and gladiator shows in the name of the emperor. Some benefactors give donations toward worship of other deities and distribute grain and oil for the poor, all so their own power grows, and the people of the city often become loyal to them.

Hostess Nympha in Laodicea

The views of people here about gods and about emperor worship easily deter people from turning to Christ. On the birthday of Caesar Augustus, there is a holiday with games in honor of the emperor and of Roma or of another pagan god. Sacrifices provide meat and festive food and entertainment for the whole neighborhood, so everyone's neighbors are wrapped up in celebrations. If Christians stay away from games and feasts, they are labeled antisocial, and, in some places, mobs attack them. The persecution for failing to worship the emperor does not always come from the emperor's edict, but often from local people who want status from their public activities. So, religious persecution is often not really about religion, but about politics.

We in Nympha's household are all Anatolians, and some are educated in Greek, or at least have a listening understanding. More than three hundred years ago, Alexander conquered many territories and introduced Greek, and now, although we have distant control from Rome, Greek is the language of education and writing. That is how Nympha comes to have a Greek-sounding name.

A few wealthy, educated women have become influential, like some in Pisidia who were against Christ and some in Macedonia and Greece who have encouraged the way of Christ. Nympha is influential, too, as a householder, although she was one of the first to follow Christ when the friends came over from Colossae. She has property and education, so people listen. She allowed us in the household to listen to the teaching from the Colossae friends and Epaphras. This was only about twenty-five years after Jesus died and rose. Some of us believed quite soon. Others hesitated. Changing one's faith is always going to bring divisions in families. Nympha understood and simply invited us to join the singing and praying and teaching in the upstairs room at the end of the week of work.

For me personally, it was a question. Women often do not step out ahead of their husbands or parents in religious matters. But Deniz was willing to listen to the teaching, too, and in a while we agreed. So did shepherd Hakan and shepherdess Ceren. Hakan's wife died years ago in childbirth. Dilara and Elif are both married, and we are praying for their husbands. We heard that Christians are baptized in water, and, when Nympha was to be baptized, we all, full of joy, accepted her invitation and were baptized along with her. We walked down to the Lycus River together, and Philemon from Colossae baptized us. We grouped together and sang songs as we came up the hill again.

That made us even more united. We welcome neighbors to join our time of worship. We hold household prayer for the day as soon as the sun rises, and once a week a longer spell, by daylight on Sunday afternoon, leaving before sunset so people reach home before it is fully dark. We invite other shepherds and shepherdesses, graziers who spend long days in the hills above the city. We invite wool washers, spinners, weavers, and tailors. If we have paying guests, we invite them, too. A few of the bankers and shop owners attend at times. They are more self-contained, though, as their money helps them feel secure without Christ.

Christians have a habit of giving great welcomes to one another. Paul teaches this in his letters. He said a Christian woman should be "well known for her good deeds, such as bringing up children, showing hospitality, washing the feet of the Lord's people, helping those in trouble and devoting herself to all kinds of good deeds." Paul even said not to view men or women as spiritual leaders unless they are hospitable. Peter, too, asks Christians to "offer hospitality to one another without grumbling." Another of our Christian leaders said, "Do not forget to show hospitality to strangers, for by so doing some people have shown hospitality to angels without knowing it." Can you imagine that?

Christians have become known for their hospitality and good deeds. Nympha and all of us care for the sick and help the poor or persecuted or imprisoned. We welcome Jews and non-Jews and dine together in a way that was previously unheard of. Here in Laodicea, we try to live by the new concept *koinonia,* fellowship. It means the warm communication between members of a house church with one another and with others, and the warm communication these people have with God.

Nympha is a remarkable leader for us. If you judged by her name, which means water fairy, you might think she is lightweight and easily influenced. That is not our Nympha. She has courage. She could not lead a church in her house without that in this unsympathetic environment. She also has initiative and faith. Even starting the group needed a sense of vision to worship the one true God and to enable and encourage others. She runs a church in a city that sees Christians as a disruptive minority worshiping a God most citizens do not want. That takes courage. She needed to feel God was leading her to do this, and the task called for the ability to stand firm when, as the householder, she would be responsible to any civil authorities or even to neighbors who might not like her worshiping or calling together a religious gathering that did not concern the emperor or even the local gods. Nympha also uses her personal resources for God, starting with her house. That is another characteristic we admire.

We have learned to like the way Nympha remains in cooperation and community with other churches, too. We often send messengers back and forth between us and Hierapolis and Colossae.

Nympha also provides a sense of family. We find Jesus taught this, too, in a different way from most Jews. The Jewish view of family turns inward. Members tend to think, "We're in a hostile environment. Let's make sure we stick together and help each other." They love their stance as inheritors of status before God, traced back to Abraham, Isaac, and Jacob and inherited from father to son. They rarely think of offering God's benefits to others.

In contrast, Jesus taught a whole new view of family. He demonstrated welcome at table to both Jews and non-Jews. Eating together indicates friendship, appreciation, and the disappearance of considerations like "one up, one down" status. Jews used to say "brother" only to a person who was a blood relative, but Jesus welcomed all his followers as if they were members of his family. He described them with the names of family relationships, such as when his mother and his brothers came. Standing outside, they sent for him. "Who are my mother and my brothers?" he asked. "Whoever does God's will is my *brother and sister and mother*." Jesus took the idea of blood relationship, applied it to anybody committed to serve God, and made it even more important than one's flesh-and-blood family. This was shocking to the people around us.

One day, we heard pounding on the door shortly after dark. Deniz went downstairs to call through the latch hole.

"Who is it?"

"It's Karamat and Asil from Colossae. We've just come on horseback and have our horses at the hitching post," they called.

Deniz welcomed them and called as he undid the chain, "What brings you here so late? Do come in and eat. We'll take your horses around to the stable."

"It's something very special. A letter from Brother Paul. He wrote to our fellowship and to Philemon and asked for the letter to be read to your church, too."

"That's exciting. A real letter from Paul, even though he has never visited our churches here in the Lycus valley? How did it come?"

THE PEOPLE PAUL ADMIRED

"You know Paul's assistant Tychicus? Paul sent him to Ephesus with a letter for the churches there, and letters for us in the Lycus. He and another man who was with Paul have just walked all the way up the valley."

"Excellent. Do come in. We'll prepare a bed-place for the night for you."

Deniz brought the two men up, and they all talked with Nympha, who immediately started to plan to send for everyone to be sure to come the next afternoon. So, the following day after prayers and hymns, we all sat ready for the letter addressed to Colossae to be read to us, too. Paul must have felt the needs were similar. There is so much movement up and down the valley that, even from Ephesus and then in Rome, Paul was hearing news of us and was keen to pass on his wisdom.

Paul wanted our churches to know Christ more keenly as the one who was "before all things, and in him all things hold together." Some people were attempting to impose restrictions such as keeping the Jewish Sabbath, worship of angels, self-denying rules about food and sex, and Jewish circumcision. Paul did not want us falling into those traps. He also taught us not to be superstitious or tied to food rituals. He wrote that, as new creatures in Christ, we should respect Jews, Gentiles, circumcised or uncircumcised, Barbarians, Scythians, slaves, and free people as equal and worthy of equal dignity. He knew it worked.

"That's what Nympha taught us, isn't it?" Elif commented. "No divisions of race or status, free or slave."

No division! Love and kindness for all! We faced working that out even more clearly a few months later. There was an earthquake. Many houses and shops fell, and, because they were stone, many people were trapped under rubble. Our "Christian family" group helped everyone they could.

"Let me pry this stone off with my crowbar," Hakan said, endeavoring to lever aside big stones of our neighbors' house.

"We'll help," rushed in Elif, while Dilara ran for blankets and drinking water.

Hakan and some of his friends carried two injured men and three children by stretcher to Nympha's house where Ceren set up a care room with sheepskins on the floor, fresh cold water, soup, and warm covers for those who may have suffered from shock.

That was only the start. Something amazing happened in Laodicea that year. Christians set such an example that the whole community pulled together, serving one another. They were already an independent lot and wealthy. Now, they added outstanding community spirit. After the earthquake, the citizens of Laodicea refused offers of help from Rome. They rebuilt their city themselves.

TWENTY YEARS LATER

I told about our city Laodicea and patron Nympha as we were years ago. It was an exciting start to our church, and what happened after the earthquake turned out to demonstrate how much Christ had changed us. We have had good and not-so-good times in the years since. I am glad to say Jesus knew all about it. It is better to be rebuked than ignored. Brother John's revelation from God included letters to seven churches here in Asia, and ours was one. The letter drew on local knowledge. God showed him how to write a message that could point right at us.

He wrote that our thinking here is: "I am rich; I have acquired wealth and do not need a thing." Some of our members are bankers on the highway in the middle of the commercial traffic. It is true. We too easily rely on ourselves, not God. God knew we were in fact "wretched, pitiful, poor, blind and naked." He told us not to buy fake gold of wealth and possessions, but the true gold of faith in him.

Jesus knew we took pride in our fashionable clothes, so he told us to buy from him white clothes to hide the nakedness of our failures. Jesus also knew about our doctors and told us to buy from him salve to put on our eyes so we can truly see how wrong we are. Jesus even used our lukewarm aqueduct water as a picture of us—all our energy and enthusiasm tempered down until Jesus was ready to vomit. What an insult! But, it was justified. Well, as I said, rebuke is better than being ignored. Jesus told us, "Those whom I love I rebuke and discipline." Then he said something that reminded me of the long years of hospitality in our church. He said it was as if he stood knocking at our door, and he painted a wonderful picture of how we could return to feeling fully warmed in his love: "If anyone hears my voice and opens the door, I will come in and eat with them and they with me." The Lord Jesus wants to dine with us in a lingering conversational meal, not a quick breakfast snack. This is deep fellowship in a rich atmosphere of hospitality. Oh, I would like that again.

THE PEOPLE PAUL ADMIRED

READER REFLECTION

When you finish reading the chapter on Nympha, imagine you are a shepherd or a merchant member of her house church. In what ways might going to the church in her home help you? Is your home like this for others?

SPEAKER/LISTENER EXPLORATION

If you used the chapter on Nympha to speak to a group, list ways in which she would be able, in the atmosphere of community, to give life-giving encouragement to individuals. What lessons can you draw from the letter twenty years later?

5

Upper-Class Philemon and Apphia in Colossae

The New View of Social Class

MAIN SCRIPTURE SOURCES: Philemon, Colossians

*P*AUL WROTE LETTERS FROM *prison in Rome to the church in Colossae and to Philemon and Apphia in about AD 58 to 60. Tychicus, originally from this area, carried these, and probably two other letters, to the churches in Philippi and Ephesus. Paul had not visited Colossae, but had learned much about it and the warmth of the people from his friend now with him in Rome, Epaphras, who founded the Colossian church. Tychicus, the courier, would be an excellent one to describe what he may have learned about Philemon and Colossae.*

Onesimus and I set out from Rome in summertime, when the sea winds are moderate, on a journey of approximately forty days. Brother Paul had charged me with four important letters in my leather scrip, my carrying case for scrolls, and the additional responsibility of escorting slave Onesimus back to his owner in Colossae. I was happy to fulfill this trust. We voyaged by Roman galley south past Sicily, east across the Ionian Sea, and north to Philippi, where I delivered my first letter to the church there. Next, we sailed eastward across the Aegean Sea and landed at Ephesus on the coast of Asia to deliver the second letter.

Now, Onesimus and I are trudging the one hundred miles up the broad valley of the Meander River in the scorching sun. Even with the well-paved Roman road, it will take us more than five days. We walk in the early morning, rest after lunch, and walk again late in the afternoon, worrying more about people to whom they are addressed and the contents of my letters than about the place where we are or the pace we travel. One of my letters, which tends to criticize the addressees, is to a church I do not know, and the other, just as sensitive, concerns the return of a slave with the hope that he would be accepted as a brother. Here with me is the slave himself, Onesimus.

"How are you feeling about this, Onesimus?" I ask.

"Hmm. I wish I could know what is going to happen, Tychicus. I did wrong in running away from Master Philemon, but, in Rome, I was far away from him and could have stayed away. Now I'm returning to offer to work for him again, unpaid. Paul thought I owed this to Master Philemon, but some of the time I ask myself, 'Why on earth am I doing this?'"

"I wonder about that, too. I must say, I respect you for coming back to put things right."

"Yes, I accepted that. But what sort of reception will we get? Does Philemon believe the same as Paul on Christian equality? What if he claps my feet in irons, incarcerates me in prison, manacles my hands, and throws away the key?"

"A master could burn a brand on your body."

"Yes. Although many slaves have become free men, I never saw Philemon allow that. It's not common in the Lycus Valley as it is in cities. I wish I knew what Philemon thinks about slavery now that he has become a believer. Are you sure he is a believer?"

"Oh, not a doubt. You know how Epaphras, who is a native of the Lycus Valley himself, is so close to Paul and in prison with him. Think how he is always wrestling in prayer for the people of the valley and tells how much the people there love God and love others because they have the Holy Spirit in them. That is what's happening there, and Philemon is one of the leaders. Epaphras knows the scene. You and your former master both love the same Jesus now."

"But what is Paul telling Master Philemon in the letter? Were you there when the letter was dictated?"

"Yes, I was there. I don't mind explaining to you, as you will know it all soon enough when it is formally read out to Philemon. It amazed me how concerned Paul was that Philemon and Apphia should treat you as a Christian brother, and yet, he could not guess how they would receive you. Paul and Philemon met and worked together for only a short time in

Upper-Class Philemon and Apphia in Colossae

Ephesus when he was teaching there. He voices the strongest argument he could think of in the letter, doing everything he can think of to persuade. He prays for Philemon and Apphia, praises them, appeals to them, and shows his love for them.

"At one stage in the letter, he even argues from his age, begging a favor of Philemon. He says, 'Your love has given me great joy and encouragement. . . . I prefer to appeal to you on the basis of love. It is as none other than Paul—an old man and now also a prisoner of Christ Jesus.'"

"Does he really say that?"

"Yes, sure. He even calls you his son. He writes, 'I appeal to you for my son Onesimus.'"

"That's encouraging."

"Hmmm. But, to tell you the truth, Onesimus, Paul obviously was worried. He wants a principle of equality carried out, and he cares about you who have served him in Rome. Still, Philemon would be fully within his rights to beat you and chain you up permanently next to the grindstones to mill wheat and barley forever after. You ran away."

"It's too true. Paul knows it is a big favor to ask to hope for mercy."

"But you would be thrilled at the way Paul has gently pushed as hard as he can. I can't remember all the words, and the parchment has a seal on it now. Paul wrote something like 'Onesimus is my heart. When I send him, I send you my own heart. He is extremely dear to me.' And he thought you would be even dearer to Philemon as a fellow human and as a brother in the Lord. He then said, 'If you consider me a partner, welcome him as you would welcome me.'"

"That is amazing, Tychicus."

"Oh, but there was one more thing. I was still there when Paul reread the letter and felt it may yet lack something. He wanted something even more persuasive. He called for a reed and ink and added, 'If he has done you any wrong or owes you anything, charge it to me. I, Paul, am writing this with my own hand. I will pay it back.' Then he sort of nailed his wish on Philemon by saying, 'Not to mention that you owe me your very self.' I wonder whether Paul secretly hopes Philemon will give you the go-ahead to return to Paul as his assistant."

"What a kindhearted benefactor Paul has been to me. I feel a lot of hope."

"There's another thing I notice, Onesimus. Even though he is so senior, he never once pulled rank as an apostle to order Philemon to obey him. He wanted to persuade Philemon toward mercy, but never to control another human, for he believes all are equal. I try to learn from his attitude myself, but it also tells us something. Paul is not placing weight on rank, even though the whole empire runs on rank and different levels in society. The Greek philosophers who influenced so much of Roman thinking talked of democracy, but even for them it was equality among equals for the highest 10 percent. And even that has not fully filtered through in Rome. But Paul is different. He would rather treat all people as brothers and sisters. I noticed he even included Apphia and Archippus as addressees in the letter. Most men would simply write to the other man, but Paul expects other family members are part of the decision making."

It was near nightfall as we reached a village by the Meander and looked for an inn for the night. When we got out on the stony road again the next day I asked a few questions myself.

"Tell me how you look at all this as a slave, Onesimus."

"A slave can't be an equal, Tychicus. That is unheard of. That *is* slavery. About one-third of the people in the Roman Empire are slaves. Who would plant and reap and thresh and grind if not slaves? Who would cut and carry the stones for the roads and houses?"

"Yes, I can see that. After the emperor, three hundred senators. After them, a tiny number of equestrians, officials on horseback. Then decurions, Roman citizens, about one in twenty of the population, and, after that, the 'respectable' people. Below them some are free but poor tenant farmers, urban day laborers, dependents of patrons. Further down are destitute orphans and widows, the ill, and the imbeciles. Slaves are below that. Some perform responsible tasks, carry important messages and money, or tutor the sons of the rich, but they lack freedom."

"That is the question. Will I be a slave or a free man when we reach Colossae and the door of Philemon's house? Will Philemon, Apphia, and Archippus heed Paul's letter?"

We walked on past cutover barley and ripening wheat fields. The orchards on the hills were a green splash with ripening cherries and plums. A few figs had already splattered soft and seedy on the ground.

The question hung over me, too. "You know Philemon more than I do, Onesimus. What is he like?" I asked. "Is he a hard man who treats his slaves with cruelty?"

"No. Like most owners, he is not excessively harsh. But landowners in Colossae seem to think, 'I can't be a leading man without slaves.' Giving a slave his manumission is asking an owner to take a financial loss, giving up valuable economic property. Besides, Paul is asking Philemon to treat me as an equal. What a hope!"

"But, there is hope in your case. Philemon is Paul's 'dear friend and fellow worker.' The whole family is obviously hospitable, with the church meeting in their home, and with Paul able to request a place in a guest room knowing he will be welcome. In fact, the letter will be read out to everyone, slave and free, for Paul addressed the family and the church that meets in their home."

So, there we were: me with letters in my leather shoulder bag and Onesimus carrying a backload and the fear of what may happen when he reaches his master once more. Left, right, along the river. Left, right, below the olive trees. Left, right, beside stone walls and sheep gates. Left, right, past vineyards and over stone bridges. Stay at an inn. Get up and keep marching with the questions ringing through our heads: What will Philemon, Apphia, and Archippus say? How will they treat Onesimus? Will it be the end of the road for one who has failed his master? Has he any future? Will he be slave or free man?

We reached the branch in the Meander River and turned along the Lycus, past apricot trees, apple trees, goats, and shepherds. We caught sight of the city poised on the slope above, shadowed to the south by higher hills and Mount Cadmus at 8,013 feet high with its remaining splash of grubby summer snow. Tramp, tramp over the stony Roman road. Slave or free man? Slave or free man?

I recalled what Epaphras told me of the Colossian church that meets in Philemon's house. Will that tell me any more about Philemon and Apphia? This couple did not found the church. That was Epaphras, who still cares much for the churches in Hierapolis, Laodicea, and Colossae, and continues praying for them in Rome. There was another possible insight there.

"Listen to this, Onesimus. I think the people in the church are particularly outgoing. Paul told them he had heard of their faith in Christ Jesus and their love for all his people. Epaphras said the gospel was bearing fruit and growing from the day they heard it, with much love in the Spirit. I'm thinking, surely, if they are a loving church, this must have had much to do with their host and hostess, Philemon and Apphia.

"Then, there were some doctrinal issues in the Colossian church. Perhaps it was Philemon who sent Epaphras to Paul to get advice.

THE PEOPLE PAUL ADMIRED

Epaphras said much was going particularly well, but then told Paul about the people there who give some teaching that sounds initially okay, but then it becomes clear that it is off at a tangent.

Were you there when Paul discussed it, Onesimus? The teaching was not pagan, for it required circumcision, special days on the calendar, and keeping the Sabbath. So it was more like Jewish belief. But it had a great many ascetic rules like, 'Don't handle this thing, don't taste that, don't touch the other.' People liked the mystical angle and the chance to be above others. It was elitist, and some claimed to reach 'fullness.'"

"Tell me more about this, Tychicus. I was not a Christian when I was in Colossae."

"Paul wrote that Jesus Christ fulfilled everything needed. Jesus is the once-forever, for-all-people Savior. The Creator, by his death and rising, has conquered all other powers. The Colossians should not accept superstitions or local religious festivals, either. Oh, yes, there was something addressed to the church that may help you, Onesimus. Paul talked about all people 'renewed in knowledge in the image of the Creator.' All are made in the image of God. With that, no person should lack respect and dignity from others. That teaches equality. Paul lists the new equalities for Christians: Gentile and Jew, circumcised and uncircumcised, slave and free. That is the new life for all of us, including you, Onesimus. I'm back with the question. Will Philemon put that into practice?"

"Another thing, Tychicus. I've seen in Rome the kindness-and-hospitality factor among believers. They give such a warm welcome in their homes. Perhaps this will help them accept me."

"That's true. Philemon and his wife and son are given to hospitality. The whole church meets at their home. These people accept the Christian culture of love."

"But what about Paul's order in his letter to the church? 'Slaves, obey your earthly masters in everything.' I'm returning to be a slave. Paul instructs, 'Masters, provide your slaves with what is right and fair.' That leaves Philemon the master, all the same." Onesimus looked for a moment as if he might run away again. But then he groaned and resolved, "Well, I shall go through with it."

"Good for you! Because there's also the teaching of Christ about forgiveness, Onesimus. Up to seventy times seven. Philemon may choose that for you." We plod on with our question: Slave or free man? Stony road. Olive trees. Relentless blue sky. Sweaty torsos.

Upper-Class Philemon and Apphia in Colossae

"Remember Epaphras talking about Philemon, Onesimus?" I mused. "He said, 'Philemon's a Greek name, though he's from Asia. Educated people do that.' Tell me about the house."

"You'll be interested to see it, Tychicus. Philemon and Apphia are so wealthy that, besides rooms for all the family and workers, there are several guest rooms. It's on the wide terrace of the city looking north across the valley—wonderful place for a sentry to see who is coming up the valley. You look down on vineyards and a whole patchwork of grain fields and orchards. Colossae, of course, used to be more important, but the road now passes to the side."

"Did you meet Epaphras when Paul sent him?"

"No, he came after I left, but we met in Rome. He said Philemon and Apphia were among the earliest to believe and tell others. They apparently opened their home straight away."

"I had an idea about that. I'm developing a theory about believers meeting in homes," I ventured. "I think it's better than the synagogue system."

"Why is that?"

"By meeting in a home, the gathering is warmer than meeting in a public building. If the day or the night is cold, there will be a fire. If people need a snack or a drink, along come a snack and a drink. If a person needs friends, here they are."

"Yes, I feel that too. If I have had a long, hard day and come to a home-gathered church, I find company to sit with. If I want to talk later in the evening, I may sit and talk, if it seems okay with the people in the house. You can't do that if you meet in a public building like a synagogue."

"Mmm. That's what I'm getting at. We saw it in Rome and in Ephesus as we passed through, don't you think, Onesimus? In homes, the old barriers in societies evaporate. When believers meet in homes, with women and men as hosts, the barrier between Jew and Greek breaks down because they eat together. What do you think about the barrier between slaves and free people? Has it disappeared in churches where you have been?"

"Yes, that has certainly changed enormously. For me to eat with freed and freeborn women and men is remarkable. Still, humans being what they are, I don't think it has fully gone. If it had, we would not be worrying about what happens when we get to Colossae."

"Sorry. You're right. I have not experienced that myself. Well, are you still able to feel church is like family?"

"I sure am, Tychicus. Paul says he feels like a father to me and that I am a son to him, and it's true."

"I notice in the teaching we hear about Jesus that he used family-related words. In the old law, using *Father* for God is rare, but now we readily use *Father* for God. Paul uses many family relationship words in his writing—especially *father*. I even heard him say he felt like a mother. He frequently says 'brothers and sisters,' for people are like that to him. It's appealing. It draws people to faith and energizes them to bring more people. It builds ties within fellowships and across to other fellowships. We already know Philemon and Apphia are frequently in touch with Hierapolis and Laodicea across the valley and will make sure to share their letter, because they are like brothers and sisters. Well, being brothers and sisters is what we are counting on now, isn't it? You have trusted this family feeling enough to return to Philemon and Apphia. You and I know that Christian love promotes at its very essence and core a ground of equality and a huge and loving hospitality factor."

"I believe it, Tychicus. God loves me and respects me as much as anybody else in all his creation."

We paused. We were nearing the end of our journey. So, I encouraged him, "Here we go up the gradual slope to Colossae now, Onesimus. We're losing daylight, so we'll take a last night at an inn. We can walk an hour tomorrow. We are resting your life and future on a principle, but we believe it is so deep in the nature of following Christ that it will serve you well and perhaps thousands of others." Both of us took heart with that—slave and free man.

We lay on sheepskins in the corner of a tavern with other travelers that night. I know Onesimus was anxious. He tossed and turned for hours. The innkeeper's wife gave us bread and cheese in the morning with fresh water from the mountain stream. Then, I slung on my leather pouch, and Onesimus hoisted his backpack. We said little now. Past cherry trees and poppies. Up a stony shortcut. Finally, we stood at the gate of Philemon's home with its spreading household buildings and storerooms.

"Is Philemon expecting you?" asked a servant. Then came introductions and welcome.

I unwrapped the letters and stood to give the personal one to Philemon as he sat on a Roman couch wearing his white toga with its

Upper-Class Philemon and Apphia in Colossae

blue border. Apphia sat beside him and the attendant waved a large fan. Onesimus held back with eyes mesmerized on the couple. They asked me as the courier to read the letter, so I stood, held up the papyrus and read aloud, glancing up occasionally into the intense faces of Philemon and Apphia. At the end of the scroll, I saw his eyes glaze over, unfocused. What was he thinking? He murmured a few words with Apphia. She nodded. Slowly, he looked up, lifted his hand, and beckoned Onesimus. His hand rested on the young man's arm.

"You are home, Onesimus," he said. "You are one of us in every sense of the words. You belong with us. You belong to the Way. When Jesus has forgiven you, how could I not do so? I give you your manumission. You may stay here as long as you like, or leave if you wish, or return to help Paul, if that is your desire. Because of Jesus, because of your integrity in returning, and because of my friend Paul, you are a free man. You have become my brother."

Instantly, Onesimus dropped to his knees on the colored mosaic floor. Words had almost departed. Gratitude took over with one word, "*Eucharistō* (I thank you)."

Our questions were over. A slave was now a free man because of the invisible kingdom of God. I folded the papyrus and saw it stored in a leather wrap. The letter had done its task. Paul, Philemon, Apphia, and I had done our task, too, of spreading the word of freedom in Christ. And where did that come from? Jesus had successfully done his task, and we are all free.

In fact, we have no proof that Philemon and Apphia forgave Onesimus and gave him his freedom. All we have is circumstantial evidence. First, Philemon did not throw out the letter or burn it in the nearest cooking fire. He kept it, and it comes down to us nearly two thousand years later. If he had refused Paul's request, he probably would have destroyed it. Second, we have an interesting piece of history. About fifty years later (AD 110), Ignatius, Bishop of Antioch, traveled under armed guard from Syria to Rome, where he suffered martyrdom. At Smyrna, the modern Izmir, he met Christian leaders including the bishop of Ephesus, named Onesimus. Onesimus was a common name, but this is worth wondering about. Was it the same Onesimus?

THE PEOPLE PAUL ADMIRED

READER REFLECTION

When you finish reading the chapter on Philemon and Apphia, pause to consider the breaking down of class barriers in their home. In your home, what are the signs that barriers of class do not exist? Thank God for the ways in which you can practice equality for all in your home.

SPEAKER/LISTENER EXPLORATION

The hospitality of this first-century couple, Philemon and Apphia, has not gone out of fashion yet. If you used the chapter to speak to a group, attempt a list of groundbreaking social changes for that society that people would have seen in the home of this couple. Which of these are still relevant today?

6

Large-Hearted Lydia and the Roman Jailer in Philippi

Living Generously, Giving Generously

MAIN SCRIPTURE SOURCES: Acts 16:12–40, Philippians

*W*HAT WOULD LIFE BE *like for one of the first house church leaders in all Europe, in Philippi, in what was then Macedonia? Could we extrapolate from Luke's summary a picture of the households of Jewish Lydia and the Roman jailer? What if we hear from one of Lydia's textile workers, perhaps a woman called Hestia?*

Greetings. I am Hestia, trained in dyeing linen cloth. Most people wear white clothes, as dyes are expensive, but some people like colored borders, and, in district capitals like Philippi and Thessalonica, wealthy women and men like to wear a purple cloak. There is a secret formula, invented by Phoenicians on the coast of Syria. They crush part of a shellfish to extract the purple dye.[1]

I want to tell about what happened when four visiting men came to our city near the sea, with its mountains behind and fertile plains with four rivers rushing down to the coast eight miles away. They must have heard a little about our history. Near us is the plain where an historic battle took place about ninety years ago when two Roman generals, Octavian

---

1. There is still a huge pile of murex shells near the coast of Sidon, in Lebanon, the remains of the city's profitable trade in purple dye two thousand years ago.

and Antony, conquered two other Romans, Brutus and Cassius. Because of that, our city became a Roman colony, and more Romans came ten years later. After another battle, more retired soldiers stayed on. Use of the Latin language grew. Eighty percent of the writings on the stones of the town forum and on tombs and markers are in Latin.

New arrivals like Paul and his friends notice that being a Roman colony has almost obliterated our mother tongue from public notices, but there are advantages for us. We have Italian law, do not pay taxes to Caesar, and are proud of our Roman heritage. This rule of law, not just street power, made all the difference later for Paul and his party.

Imagine these four men just arrived from Asia: two Jews, one Gentile, and, I learned later, one who is half Jewish. As in other Roman cities, they saw the marketplace with stone shops and a central open space about one hundred yards by fifty yards, the *forum*. On the northern side stands a stone platform for a judge to try law cases, surrounded by stone porches, temples, and public buildings fronting the open space. A thousand-foot-high citadel or castle rock, *acropolis*, towers over the forum.

Our city is accustomed to visitors. The men walked about without hindrance. They were well traveled and educated and could soon guess there were few Jews—not even the standard ten men necessary for a synagogue—and that anti-Jewish feeling could erupt quickly. They saw that later. Paul, Luke, Silas, and Timothy hiked along the famous straight road, the Egnatian Way, which runs north/south through the city.

The roads are important, bringing traders and goods. That is how I have a job. My boss is a trader from Thyatira in Anatolia across the Aegean Sea. Lydia is her name, naturally enough, as there is a town called Lydia near Thyatira, another textile town with guilds of dyers. Roman law allows a widow only one-tenth of her husband's assets, but fathers can give dowries and inheritance to daughters, money they can keep, that never goes into their husband's family coffers. So, Lydia got started with money from her own family, and she has done well running her own business. We follow the common Greek and now Roman system of living as part of her household. A female head of the household is not common, but it does occur. We join her family, slaves, free workers, official friends, clients, and, at times, visiting traders.

Lydia was a God-fearer, attracted to the Jewish faith, but not born into it. She invited us in the household and some other women to go with her to a prayer meeting on Saturdays. She welcomed us, saying,

"We don't work on Saturday anyway. Feel free to join us by the Gangites River to pray."

"Sure, Madam," I replied. "I like learning new things." I went with her and the others out of the city through the arch that stretches over the Egnatian Way and turned northwest to the Gangites about one and a half miles out. We washed our hands at the riverbank before prayers. We went there often, learning about the God who made the world, and learning to sing and pray to this God.

One Saturday, these four polite men located our prayer meeting and joined us. They said they could not find a synagogue here, but heard about our gathering for people who fear God. They told us much more about the Living God than we had known, and about Jesus, the Anointed One who died for humans and then became alive again. They talked all afternoon, and we felt wonderfully enlightened and believed their good news about Jesus Christ.

"You can identify with Jesus and symbolically die to your old life by being dipped in water," the leader, Paul, said. "You can rise up to new life as a follower of Christ." Of course, the Gangites was right there.

The teaching made sense and spoke to our hearts, yet still we watched almost frozen in place when Lydia said, "Let me do it. I want to become a true follower of Christ. I believe he is the Son of God, and we already worship God. Now we know how to be free from our sins." We watched. Silas, Paul's companion teacher, trod into the water, and then Lydia, pressing down her gown to make it wet. I heard the words, "I baptize you in the name of the Father, the Son, and the Holy Spirit." He gently dipped her under the water. It was not out of character for her. She was a woman of faith and courage and had clearly moved on to further knowledge of the same God, but it was a huge sign of change.

"That's my household head," I thought. "I can't conceive of anyone I would rather work for, but, let me think. . . . Yes, I have learned to worship and trust Jehovah God. Now I learn that his Son Jesus died and lived again. He can forgive what I have done wrong. The Son of God can be my companion in life."

Paul asked, "Does anyone else understand and want to make a statement that they will serve Jesus?" Some fellow workers stood up to join Lydia.

"Yes, she has their loyalty," I thought. But, immediately, I mentally added, "It's more than loyalty. I know them so well. It is not out of character for them, either. They have learned their devotion to the One God from Lydia. I have heard their earnest prayers so often." Then my friend Ilona stepped into the water. Suddenly, I knew what to do. I, too, jumped up and walked into the river. I felt the water over my knees, up to my waist, and cool over my head and shoulders, with the words of commitment to Jesus, to his Father, and to the Holy Spirit ringing over my head. But, in my chest, my heart was warm. "I do want to thank you, Jesus Christ. I do choose you. Let me live a new life for you."

The next thing I heard was Lydia inviting the visitors to leave their inn and stay at the household. "If you consider me a believer in the Lord, come, and stay at my house," she persuaded. She is like that—generous herself, and generous with her home. Jews do not like staying in inns anyway; inns have a reputation for low morals, dirt, and bedbugs. When I heard them say, "Thank you, Lydia. We would be so happy to come," I hurried home to light the sticks in the clay stove and prepare some soup and flatbread.

The household system colors much of our lives. It is broader than a couple and their children, or even their parents, brothers, and sisters. Lydia found when she read the Greek version of the old law that Jews in Palestine who could afford it often had additional people in the home. The custom even shows in the old law books: "You, your sons and daughters, your male and female servants, and the Levites from your towns who have no allotment or inheritance of their own." Being included gives protection and standing to many people. People do not live as singles, or even as a couple. When servants and slaves live in with a family, the family head is responsible for their behavior and can give physical punishment, but is also responsible for their wellbeing, protection, shelter, warm clothes, and food, and argues for their legal rights. Belonging to a household gives a place in society so that slaves cannot be abused. Here and in Rome, it is called a *familia*.

The four travelers, Paul, Silas, Dr. Luke, and the younger man Timothy, stayed as temporary members of our *familia*. I had to keep my dyeing vats working and hang the yarn and cloth out to dry, and my fellow workers kept up the spinning, weaving, and stitching. Sometimes, rich people came to the front room to buy purple braid or purple-bordered cloaks. Sometimes, we all helped a buyer bundle up a pack-load for a mule. Luke and Timothy came out and helped while Paul and Silas did more teaching. I loved the new teaching and all the friendship and encouragement between the prayer group and the traveling religious teachers. They taught us in the house and courtyard and out along the stone-slab road toward the prayer point.

On several days, we saw a troubled slave-girl fortune-teller shouting, "These men are servants of the Most High God who are telling you the way to be saved." Our new household members guessed her owners made money through her, but they were accustomed to anti-Jewish feeling in many cities. They ignored her. Healing her could trigger an anti-Jewish disturbance. Still, Paul felt troubled. Perhaps he was upset that, when she said Paul and the others served the Most High God, most people would think she meant Zeus, called Jupiter in Latin.

Or, perhaps he was upset at the system that could exploit and manipulate a girl so severely, as well as at the noise she persistently made. She was at the bottom of all social scales, and they treated her inhumanely—abused slave, female, young, emotionally disturbed, and bad mannered as well. Why would a supposedly proud Jew care about this non-Jew? Besides, this unfortunate woman was powerless, no advantage to anyone except for her fortune telling. A slave was property. To act for the advantage of a disenfranchised slave looked like interfering with another's property. Paul knew this, too. There was money involved. Tempers flare when people lose money. He delayed, perhaps aware of the danger to himself and his friends, but, eventually, he knew he must challenge the abuse. Paul turned and sternly commanded the evil spirit, "In the name of Jesus Christ, I command you to come out of her." The spirit immediately left her.

Sure enough, when their income was at risk, the girl's owners stirred up an anti-Jewish demonstration, street action, and a riot. Officers took Paul and Silas to the magistrate's judgment seat, stripped and shamed them, flogged them, and threw them into prison in an inner cell with their feet in stocks.

The astounding thing for me was finding the next morning after an earthquake that the jailer has been converted in the night and was genuinely a changed man. From locking their feet in wooden stocks one day, as I heard, by the next morning he was personally washing the cuts and bruises on the backs of Silas and Paul. The jailer's household, with wife, sons, daughters, in-laws, cooks, maids, gardeners, and prison warders followed their household head, just as I had followed Lydia. They believed in Jesus the Christ.

THE PEOPLE PAUL ADMIRED

Now, there were two households of Christ-believers in our city: ours with Lydia, a small group with primarily Jewish thinking, and the jailer's household with its Greek and Roman background. I was thoroughly astounded at the turn of events—our new teachers freed, and more than twenty new believers in Christ.

I know people feel pride here in our Roman law, though few are imperial citizens. Some have citizen status, and some are freed slaves. So, when teacher Paul suddenly revealed that he is an imperial freeborn citizen, the big men in the city were horrified. They had treated a Roman citizen in an illegal way! They had not given Paul a trial; they had tied him and put him in stocks; they had beaten him. He should not have been manhandled, certainly not flogged, nor imprisoned without trial. He had the right to appeal to the high court in Rome. The terrified magistrate told the jailer to let them go immediately, but Paul announced to the officers, "They beat us publicly without a trial, even though we are Roman citizens, and threw us into prison. And now they want to get rid of us quietly? No! Let them come themselves and escort us out."

The magistrates begged for mercy. Their own heads could roll. Their offices and the free status of the city colony were at risk. Ever so politely, they escorted Paul and Silas from the prison and requested them to leave town.

Paul found lessons for our church and us over that later. He asked us all to believe we are nothing less than first-class citizens when it comes to the kingdom of God. He wrote, "But our citizenship is in heaven," and urged us to live up to the standards of the high citizenship we already own as believers in Christ, even when we suffer ill treatment and persecution: "Whatever happens, as citizens of heaven live in a manner worthy of the gospel of Christ . . . without being frightened in any way by those who oppose you."

Meanwhile, Lydia invited everyone to meet at her place before Paul left, and this time I blinked as I looked around. I asked myself, "Am I seeing things? Here is Lydia's household of Macedonian Greek-speaking women and men, with Lydia, who can also speak the language of Thyatira, and Paul, a Jewish rabbi who is also, surprisingly, a Roman citizen. Here are some of his Jewish and Gentile friends, including a half-Jew, a Latin-speaking jailer and his wife and their servants, more Latin speakers such as jail warders, and a Macedonian girl who was demon possessed. But look at Lydia's big heart. She made us all feel at home at her place and at home with each other. One word described us all: *believers*. The visiting teachers gave us all such a motivational talk that we felt stronger. We had already experienced stress and fear together.

Paul left, going south to Thessalonica, and, in a short while, Lydia's generous nature influenced us all. We heard that the synagogue people in Thessalonica had treated Paul and his friends harshly. "That's so hard on them all," Lydia said. "Let's show them we care. Who would like to help with a collection from savings and wages and make up a bag of money to send?" Many of us did just that.

We found out in a letter to our church years later that this meant a huge amount to Paul. He wrote, "As you Philippians know, in the early days of your acquaintance with the gospel, when I set out from Macedonia, not one church shared with me in the matter of giving and receiving, except you only; for even when I was in Thessalonica, you sent me aid more than once when I was in need."

I asked myself some questions. Who first set our church the example of a warm and caring prayer cell? Who set the example of generous welcome to visiting Christian teachers? Who had the church come back to her place as soon as new people were added? It was Lydia with her heart-warming personality.

GROWING THE PHILIPPI CHURCH

The first time we met for prayer after Paul and his friends left, we all paused, wondering what language we should use. Not the Aramaic of Palestine, and nobody spoke the Hebrew of the Scriptures we had been reading. Around us, most people spoke Greek, even if they had a Macedonian patois as well. But, the jailer and his leading servants spoke Latin. No wonder we were confused. So, as a compromise, we chose the more generally known Greek.

The people from the jailer's household did not know the Hebrew songs we had learned by living in Lydia's household. Indeed, they knew almost nothing about the One True God. They did not know him as Creator, Provider, Almighty, or as a Father. They had hardly heard of the Holy Spirit. We in Lydia's household had at least some of the Jewish background of Christian faith, including its ethical teaching, but they were starting from scratch without such God-fearing ethics. We taught the jailer's household members some songs, taught them how to pray, and especially how to worship a God they could not see. That initially made no sense to them, for they had always prayed to images.

We were happy to help, so we worked hard to coach this large household of Greek and Latin people to understand enough from Jewish, and now Christian, faith for them to understand about Jesus. Two educated women and one man did much of the teaching: Euodia, Synteche, and Clement. Lydia joined them to teach discipleship and prayer, as she was responsible for anything in her house. Some of the teaching was new to us, but the number of new concepts needed in the jailer's household was mind-blowing. They needed new ethics and morality, honesty, faithfulness in marriage, anger management, and getting away from the drinking habits of so many Roman officers.

I made friends with some from the jailer's household. Portia is a housekeeper, and her husband Cassius a prison warder. They told me, "The commander is a changed man. We would not believe it if we did not see it with our own eyes. He was pitiless and brutal. Look how severely he flogged Paul and Silas. His callousness got him the job as chief officer of the whole prison.

"He was told to guard those two men closely, so he put them in the innermost cell with their feet in stocks. He had to cover his own back, for, if prisoners escaped, his own life was on the line. When he thought the prisoners had escaped, he nearly committed suicide with the sword he always kept by him. His pride as a Roman required that. Paul guessed it, too, and shouted to him in the dark not to harm himself. Now, this man, so hard and unfeeling, turns out to have a sensitive core that can be touched.

"He actually trembled. He fell on his knees shaking all over in front of Paul and Silas, and then he listened and had others in the household listen as Paul taught about Jesus. Suddenly, he became kindhearted in a way we never would have dreamed possible. God must have done it. The hard-as-nails Roman commander asked how to be saved.

"He so wanted change that he made us and many others in the household get up and listen to Paul right then in the night. Before morning light, he gently brought Silas and Paul into his house, personally washed the whip cuts on their backs, and got a delicious meal brought to them. Our eyes were popping out with surprise.

"He must already have heard of baptism. Next thing, he asked if he could be baptized and asked us if we wanted to join him. We had no

Large-Hearted Lydia and the Roman Jailer in Philippi

objections. If this good news could change a pitiless man into someone who would wash the wounds of prisoners and provide them a decent meal before dawn, we wanted it, too. That dawn glowed almost like a party; the jail commander was so delighted and happy that he had believed in God along with all his family."

Portia and Cassius say the household has become nearly unrecognizable in comparison with its past. Euodia, Synteche, and Clement joined them often to teach more about Christ and how to follow him. The household members learned not to bother about spells and charms. They stopped living in fear of bad luck and dread of gods who could visit bad fortune on them. Fortune-tellers no longer mattered. They ignored city feast days when they could. They prayed without relying on a pagan priest. They live their lives now with joy, for things are so different.

Gradually, the church numbers in Philippi grew, for people invited their friends, and Clement, Euodia, Synteche, and Lydia taught them, too. After the jailer's people had joined with our household to learn for a while, the jailer started a house church in his home near the jail because numbers were increasing. He turned into such a considerate and kind man that people feel drawn to him as a man transformed by Christ.

The young woman from whom Paul threw out the evil spirit needed a place to stay, so Lydia invited her into the household. She soon fit in and joined us with weaving and sewing. Our church in Lydia's house is remarkable. There is, quite simply, a load of love to go around. Paul visited twice more about three years later and became so familiar with our group that he believes our love for one another can attract more people to Jesus. He said, "Let your gentleness be evident to all." He praised Euodia and Synteche, saying they had "contended at my side in the cause of the gospel, along with Clement and the rest of my coworkers." In fact, when the two women differed after working together extremely well for years, I felt pleased that Paul begged them to bury their differences and cooperate happily again. I like the fact that Paul can trust our group to draw them into the warmth again. He wrote, "Help these women." Indeed, Paul counts on the love in our church to overcome any hurdles or personality differences. In my opinion, that is due to Lydia's influence. He wrote, "If you have any . . . common sharing in the Spirit, if any tenderness and compassion, then make my joy complete by being like-minded, having the same love, being one in spirit and of one mind." He knows we all love every member. He even felt it years later, imprisoned in Rome, when we

THE PEOPLE PAUL ADMIRED

sent Epaphroditus with more money for him and to inquire about his welfare.

Lydia and the jailer kept right on learning more about Jesus the Savior, welcoming more people to the house churches, and coaching them to trust the One True God and his Son Jesus Christ. All the new people belong in the circle of warmth and fellowship. Paul prayed confidently, "He who began a good work in you will carry it on to completion until the day of Christ Jesus." I believe it. I say a loud "Amen" to Paul's prayer, "That your love may abound more and more in knowledge and depth of insight, so that you may be able to discern what is best and may be pure and blameless for the day of Christ." Our first church leaders, Lydia and the jail commander, will always support that.

READER REFLECTION

When you finish reading the chapter on Lydia and the jail commander, take time to contemplate the meaning of generosity of spirit. Ask God to show you ways to make generosity of spirit part of your personality.

SPEAKER/LISTENER EXPLORATION

If you used the chapter on Lydia and the jail commander to speak to a group, prepare with them a list of potential problems between the two households and discuss the Christian way of overcoming them. What had generosity to do with the story?

7

Jason Takes Responsibility in Thessalonica

Relationships that Reach Out

OTHER LEADERS: Aristarchus, Secundus

MAIN SCRIPTURE SOURCES: Acts 17:1–10; Romans 16:21; Acts 19:29, 20:4, 27:2

*L*UKE'S REPORT OF THE *beginning of the church in Thessalonica in about AD 51 is a summary by a visitor. What would an insider like Macedonian Aristarchus perhaps be able to tell us?*

I came to know Paul well indeed during the years after his key visit to our city, so I am keen to talk. I first met him in Thessalonica. Later, my friends and I were with Paul in Ephesus during the riot over the goddess Diana. Shortly after that, Secundus, also from Thessalonica, and I traveled with Paul farther north in Macedonia, turned south toward Greece, back north to Macedonia, and then Paul sent us and a few others ahead to Troas in Asia where he met us again. More than two years after that, I was with Paul and Luke on the ship going to Rome and then imprisoned with him there.

Back when Paul, Timothy, and Silas left suddenly from Lydia's home in Philippi, they hurried southwest about a hundred miles on the Egnatian Way through the next two towns, Amphipolis and Apollonia. They stopped when they reached Thessalonica, on its large gulf on the Aegean Sea within sight of 9,600-foot-high Mount Olympus. We first

THE PEOPLE PAUL ADMIRED

met Paul and his friends outside the synagogue and welcomed them to Thessalonica.

"What's special about this city?" Paul asked.

"It began about three hundred years ago to take advantage of the fine harbor for shipping and overland caravans of horses and mules traveling the Egnatian Way," I told him.

"It will suit us," Paul retorted. "I prefer to teach in cities on trade routes with well-built Roman roads. That way, our good news travels farther."

"Then you will like it here, Paul. Thessalonica is the chief city of Macedonia. Since Emperor Octavian made it a free city, it has kept its Greek republican government, mints its own coins, and does not have a Roman garrison inside its walls. Still, there are many Roman officials, and alongside them a few thousand Jews, many of them merchants. I note you speak Greek. The majority of the more than 200,000 people are Greek, and the leading culture is Greek—different from the Latin upper echelons of Philippi. Many Greeks have become God-fearers, honoring your Jewish God."

"That's good. We'll start telling the gospel in the synagogue. Is society like it is in the other cities influenced by Greece and Rome?"

"Yes, it is. Most upper-class people view those who work with their hands as uneducated and lacking in virtue, but there are large numbers of them, and the city would not function without them. Lining the streets are the shops of weavers, potters, fullers, barbers, bakers, butchers, booksellers, blacksmiths, cobblers, sculptors, and moneylenders. Proud of their skills, they work from sunrise to sunset with two hours of rest after lunch. Sons and some daughters become apprentices, and many people take the name of their trade, like smith, baker, or weaver. There is friendly competition between the shops of the same trade in a market street."

We showed Paul some of the older part of town where streets were a normal part of the living space. Men lounged outside taverns, women sat on steps checking the children's heads for lice, and more children ran about with a ball in a game of tag. Women lined up at a stone water pipe waiting turns with their clay pitchers—a good opportunity to chat about their cooking or the need for more stones around the muddy tap. A porter or two brought a backload of wood or fresh supplies of wool for spinning. Some of the women spun in a corner of daylight against a building, and a tailor stitched clothes in a recess that was merely a hole in the wall. With

Jason Takes Responsibility in Thessalonica

local knowledge, I guided Paul to center-street as a ragged man passed with a large clay pot of night-soil to be taken outside to the fields. The shallow stone drain was already grimy with refuse.

Our visitors paused to take in the scene: ordinary people struggling for food, water, health, harmony. Life is hard on so many. Paul and Timothy decided to use the services of a street barber with his large sharpened blade. It fell to me to stand guard, preventing the usual jostling in that particular corner. It has happened that jostling a barber has caused a serious cut.

"I have a message for all these people," Paul commented. "I would love to bring to them to faith in Jesus Christ, who died so they could live a purposeful life as followers of the living God. They would also find peace, joy, and cleanliness. I shall give the Jews the first chance, and then offer the good news to these ordinary Gentile people."

Paul taught from the Scriptures at the synagogue three Saturdays in a row. He worked hard to convince the people there. You could say his theme song was, "The Messiah had to suffer and rise from the dead. This Jesus I am telling you of is the Messiah." However, the synagogue leaders put Paul out after those three weeks. In spite of this, a man called Jason accepted that Christ was the Messiah and invited Silas, Paul, and Timothy to carry on teaching from his home. The gospel spread rapidly among a few from the synagogue and the Jewish community. Soon, a great many more God-fearing Greeks believed in Jesus. In fact, numbers grew spectacularly. We saw lives transformed, even though it was a hard road personally for many of them. Paul wrote later that the people in Thessalonica "welcomed the message in the midst of severe suffering with the joy given by the Holy Spirit." They "turned to God from idols to serve the living and true God."

We saw the changes. Some had in their houses small statues to worship. When they rejected these gods and put them outside the city, some citizens became outraged. "What do you think you're doing?" they shouted.

"Is this how you treat a god?" bellowed another. "Get out there this minute and bring them back. And don't forget the bathing ritual. Then you'll have to garland them with flowers and bring a serious votive offering."

Jason and the other new believers said nothing.

THE PEOPLE PAUL ADMIRED

"What? You're not bringing them back?" another citizen screamed. "This is not only about you. If you dishonor the gods, you bring bad luck on all of us. There will be plague, famine, and earthquakes. You'll ruin us."

"I'm sorry to upset you," Jason spoke calmly. "We believe these stone statues are exactly that, and not more than stone statues. Nevertheless, there is a high God over the entire world and he loves us. Let me tell you some more...."

What turmoil followed! Antipathy, anger, and opposition came from the synagogue. From non-Jews came outrage, persecution, and disturbances on the streets. The believers back in Philippi heard about it and twice sent financial assistance, in addition to the fact that Paul worked night and day to maintain himself and the gospel work.

Jason spoke out clearly. "What Paul taught changed my life," he said. "As a Jew, I knew about the eternal God, but this is a vast, new scene. We all tried hard to keep the law, but Paul told us to accept the death of Jesus to make us pure enough to serve God. That was a surprise. A crucified person is a cursed person. Could such a man be the Messiah? But, it began to make sense. I accepted Jesus' sacrifice and felt I was becoming a new person. I set my heart on helping, so I invited the men of God to stay at my house."

Paul was thrilled with the response here. He wrote later, "The Lord's message rang out from you not only in Macedonia and Achaia—your faith in God has become known everywhere."

After Jason offered lodging to Paul, Silas, and Timothy, many people realized they could find them at Jason's place. Visitors crowded along. Jason was thrilled. He became nearly as keen as Paul and Silas to tell our countrymen that the Messiah has come and to tell Greeks, Romans, and people from the hills that they, too, could trust in Jesus.

However, in a while, this all brought huge troubles on Jason's head, although at least he knew the legal system and what to do. I am still shocked by what some Jewish people did. They were jealous of Paul's popularity and detested him teaching this new doctrine, so they found some loafers hanging around in the market and incited them to start a riot in the city.

"Look at these disturbers of the peace," they said as they stirred up the bystanders. "They're trying to get you to worship an alien god."

"Are you about to sit there and let our gods and our Caesar be shamed?" goaded another.

Jason Takes Responsibility in Thessalonica

Before long, the leaders persuaded them to make an attack. They rushed to Jason's house to search for Paul and Silas so they could tear them limb from limb. They could not find them. Instead, they dragged out Jason and some other believers. We were all scared and felt badly persecuted.

The crowd shouted to our city officials, the politarchs, "These men who have caused trouble all over the world have now come here, and Jason has welcomed them into his house. They are all defying Caesar's decrees, saying that there is another king, one called Jesus." Of course, that put a political slant on their story. The crowd and the city officials were thoroughly confused, but they latched on to the idea of arresting Jason.

"You caused all this," they blamed him. "You are the householder. You are responsible for what happens in your house. You let the visitors under your roof cause trouble and overstep the laws on illegal association."

"It's okay," Jason replied. "We are not doing anything wrong."

"That's a debatable point," one of the politarchs cried. "It is not so harmless. Look at this riot. It happened because of the people staying in your household. That does concern you."

"It is your responsibility to make sure that does not happen again," shouted the leading politarch. "You are going to put down a significant sum of money. If your friends disturb the peace again, you lose the deposit. If you don't pay up, we keep you in custody."

Jason thought quickly and then said, "Yes, sure. I'll pay the bond. We are not the troublemakers, but I'll take responsibility for Paul and his friends' behavior."

The politarchs were only doing their job: trying to prevent another riot. Jason handed over his own cash, and they let him go. Then, he invited me and Secundus and a couple of the leading women who had contacts among the politarchs to come to his house and discuss what to do.

"I wish we could keep Paul and his friends here," Jason voiced aloud. "They are giving us such life-giving teaching."

Secundus agreed. "We are so blessed. Their coaching feels like food, it is so nourishing. But . . ." he trailed off.

Delphina, acquainted with the city leaders, took the discussion further. "The word among the politarchs is that they will not be responsible to keep the peace unless these friends leave. I think their safety and ours is at risk. The politarchs can't control the mob."

"They are probably right. What does that mean? Do we have to tell them to go?" Jason concluded.

"Yes, sorry. I'm hearing too much from the city officials. Do you mind telling them?"

Jason sadly went back to Paul, Timothy, and Silas, feeling he was hardly acting the host he wanted to be. "I'm so sorry about this, friends," he explained. "I didn't want to say this. Would you mind leaving as fast as you can? We understand that your life and property are at risk if you stay—and ours, too."

"Of course, we won't stay and endanger you," Paul and the others said. They set out as soon as it was night for Berea, which was off the beaten track and less likely to bring trouble on the heads of friends or on their own. Some people have misunderstood what happened here, thinking the city accused Paul of speaking of another king, and this got him into strife, as it is against the law to predict a change of ruler. That is partly true. However, Paul and Silas were not the ones hauled up before the politarchs, but Jason, and they called him to stand investigation for breaking the laws against voluntary associations. In previous places, Paul boldly faced his accusers, but he did not do that here in Thessalonica. Perhaps he and Jason felt it was too dangerous.

Jason gave us an example of bravery that set the churches in Thessalonica on the path of courage and integrity. He risked sneers and put-downs, yet, under him, the church thrived and grew in hospitality. Delphina analyzed it this way: "Several of us take hospitality to believers very seriously. Because we come from prominent homes, we could serve even when there was difficulty. Paul wrote of it later. 'You suffered from your fellow citizens.' 'We boast about your perseverance and faith in all the persecutions and trials you are enduring.'"

Lysandra wondered, "The first believers in the Way in Jerusalem must have done as we do here. I think hospitality is a Christian virtue. Do you agree, Delphina?"

"Oh, definitely. Luke thought so, too. He told us he saw it in Jesus' parable about attending a wedding feast, and how people should not take the highest seats for themselves."

"We take that cue here," Lysandra picked up the thread. "Jesus said, 'Invite the poor, the crippled, the lame, the blind, and you will be blessed.' We welcome people from all strata of society. Luke told us how Lydia

Jason Takes Responsibility in Thessalonica

provided food for Paul and his friends, and Paul and Silas ate food prepared by non-Jews in the Philippi jail."

The new believers had remarkable models to learn from: Jason as host, willing to give his finances over to God, and Paul for kindness. You could say Paul loved people into the kingdom. He said later, "Just as a nursing mother cares for her children, so we cared for you. Because we loved you so much, we were delighted to share with you not only the gospel of God, but our lives as well." When Paul could not see us, he said he felt like an orphan. That says it all. The message of Jesus spread through the city and across two provinces. Paul wrote later, "You yourselves have been taught by God to love each other. And, in fact, you do love all the brothers and sisters throughout Macedonia. Yet we urge you, dear friends, to do so more and more."

Paul could not revisit Thessalonica for some time, but sent Timothy, who told him we were doing well. We did not get everything right. Paul had to tell some of us friends to "mind your own business and work with your hands." When some believers died, he told us what happens after death and pointed to the far future. He visited us again on his third missionary journey, on his way to Greece, and again on his return. Secundus and I traveled with him some of the way.

Jason and the rest of us in Thessalonica felt it was true when Paul said, "We dealt with each of you as a father deals with his own children, encouraging, comforting and urging. . . ." Though Paul was not married, nobody could accuse him of not understanding family love and caring. We learned from him and Jason a love that made the gospel travel to hundreds of homes.

LATER INSIGHT

Christians later gained such a name for kindness and hospitality that people at times mocked them for it. This comes from a non-Christian source, the Roman satirist Lucian:

> From the crack of dawn on you could see grey-haired widows and orphan children hanging around the prison and the bigwigs of the sect used to bribe the jailers so they could spend the night with a Christian prisoner inside. Full-course dinners were brought to him, their holy scriptures read to him, and our excellent Peregrinus . . . was hailed as a latter-day Socrates. From as far away as Asia Minor, Christian communities sent committees, paying their

THE PEOPLE PAUL ADMIRED

expenses out of the common funds, to help him with advice and consolation. The efficiency the Christians show whenever matters of community interest like this happen is unbelievable; they literally spare nothing.[1]

READER REFLECTION

When you finish reading the chapter on Jason and the Thessalonians who loved their neighbors into the kingdom of God, consider using this prayer:

> We turn to you, our Savior, realizing Jason, Paul, Aristarchus, and the leading women offer us some remarkable role models. Jason took responsibility, and God gave him courage that inspired others. Paul loved people into following Christ Jesus with such a culture of kindness that Jason and the Christians of Thessalonica easily spoke and acted love for others. Believers offered their homes. We are impressed. Let us carry with us some mental prompting from this narrative that makes us stronger in our times. Enable us to ignore sneers and refuse to pander to respect for the wrong reasons. Enable us to suffer financial disadvantage when it is for you. Guide us when faithfulness to you could affect our income or promotion.
>
> As a believing community, even when our task is slow and hard, make us tireless in following up with people and showing love, as Jason and the Thessalonians did with such welcome and warmth. May we love people into the kingdom of God. Where we long for this, but the task is testing, help us take a page from the book of Paul, Jason, and the leading women, and refuse to give up.

SPEAKER/LISTENER EXPLORATION

If you used the chapter on Jason and the Thessalonians to speak to a group, discuss with them, perhaps using a whiteboard, the references to love for fellow believers and for neighbors, largely from 1 and 2 Thessalonians. This was nearly two thousand years ago. Ask listeners how these might work out in their twenty-first century place and time.

---

1. Lucian Peregrine 12–13, in Greer, 119–20, quoted Martin and Davids, *Dictionary*, 506.

8

Noble Leaders in Berea

Sopater and Friends Search the Scriptures

MAIN SCRIPTURE SOURCES: Acts 17:10–15, 20:4; Romans 16:21

*L*UKE WROTE A HIGHLY *abbreviated version of the missionary team's visit to Berea. Suppose Silas, also in the traveling party, wrote his version and gave a fuller picture such as the following:*

We left Philippi and then Thessalonica feeling knocked about and shaken. We knew we had a great message to tell, but would we continue to jeopardize our new friends and ourselves? We hoped as we traveled that, in the next city, people would be allowed to listen to our message in peace. As we journeyed, we talked.

I commented, "This trip is becoming increasingly significant, isn't it? We reach key cities, we teach, some believe in each place. The message will not stop there."

"Sometimes I feel as if we are just a few men riding in boats, walking on Roman roads, and getting hounded out of city after city," Timothy interjected. "We have adventures, and our message gets accepted by a few people who will ever after have trouble with the authorities in their city. Sometimes I wonder if it's more than that."

"It had better be more than that!" Paul exclaimed, nearly stumbling on an uneven stone in his anxiety to quell such a thought. "Think how Jason put his livelihood on the line in Thessalonica. Think how God has shown us each time where to go next. This is the news of the Messiah we all wanted, but the magnitude of the message has grown exponentially because it no longer applies only to Jews. We saw it change lives for God-fearing Greek men and even those wealthy women."

"Of course, it is exciting, Paul. I love coming along with you," Timothy went on. "I can't help wondering what the next adventure will be."

I'm older. I kept these thoughts to myself. But I had no idea *how* momentous this was, and *how much* would follow. That became clear later. In cities we visited, people put their faith in Jesus as Savior. Cultures and religious views started to change, local politics were affected, views of ethics changed, and even perspectives on art shifted. We were influencing Europe, and every city had its significance. Each new church leader would face large challenges. Sopater in Berea, for example, would lead a congregation taken with a deep urge to study the Scripture, and, after Paul taught in Athens, Dionysius and Damaris would lead where people preferred the latest fashions.

Pensively, we hiked farther along on the Egnatian Way to prosperous Berea on the foothills of Mount Bermium, forty-five miles southwest of Thessalonica. The city sits on the watershed ridge between the Eliakomon and Axios rivers near fertile alluvial plains. Agricultural and orchard products abound—chickpeas, olives, apples, pears, and peaches. As an established and busy city, it has fountains, theater, and a circular race track. The Jews here, about one-fifth of the population, were far more receptive than those in Thessalonica, and many believed when Paul, as usual, started his preaching and teaching in the synagogue.

Here, I first met Sopater, son of Pyrrhus. He emerged as a leader in Berea and later traveled with Paul from Macedonia to Greece and back. This was part of Paul's teaching methods: taking developing leaders along with him as advanced training. On his third missionary journey, the group grew to seven men: Sopater from Berea, Aristarchus and Secundus from Thessalonica, Gaius, Timothy, Tychicus, and Trophimus.

Paul explained in the synagogue here, as he usually does, "Jesus fulfills the prophecies of our sacred Scriptures. He is the Messiah we have all been looking for."

"Where is that in the law?" they asked. "Show us this." They unrolled scrolls, searched the parchments, and peered at the Hebrew writing. "We want to see for ourselves," the Bereans urged. What a brilliant response. Paul loved it.

Noble Leaders in Berea

"Look at this in this Isaiah scroll," Paul pointed out: "'A virgin shall conceive and bear a son.' That was Mary, the mother of Jesus." Many of them joined the new pastime of searching the Jewish Scriptures.

"Look what I've found further in the Isaiah scroll," Bion shouted. "Listen: 'He was despised and rejected by others, a man of suffering.' That sounds like your description of Christ. Oh, and listen here: 'Surely he took our pain and bore our suffering.' That is a Messiah who suffers. Not the triumphant warrior we were thinking of."

Sopater was next. "There's an excellent one in the scroll of the Psalms here: 'They divide my clothes among them and cast lots for my garments.' That's what you told us happened, Paul. Hey, this is so thrilling!"

Paul followed up with his regular teaching. "Here's more in the Psalms scroll: 'I will give you the holy and sure blessings promised to David.' What God promised our ancestors he has fulfilled for us, their children, by raising up Jesus."

Paul, Timothy, and I were all delighted as we saw the enjoyment the people in Berea had finding the prophecies. Sopater was so quick. "Here's another," he would call, and read out a passage like, "You, Bethlehem . . . out of you will come for me one who will be the ruler over Israel." So Paul would ask, "Have you found this yet? Peter quoted it when the Holy Spirit was given: 'You will not abandon me to the realm of the dead, nor will you let your faithful one see decay.' That's about Jesus not staying in the grave."

It was like a party, everyone was so eager. They met every day, rushed to the parchments, and exclaimed, "See, this proves what Paul said is true." They had enormous trust in the Scriptures. Most grew quickly in the faith because they studied them so much, and Sopater soon stood out as a leader. These Bereans were among the most Scripture-focused groups in all the churches. We all thought they showed true nobility of character. What a change for us—from being rushed away under cover of night to now speaking in public in the synagogue and Jews accepting the good news eagerly and searching the old Scriptures for confirmation. We sat for hours in the synagogue talking, searching, and studying.

A good number of Jews in Berea became believers, as did quite a big group of high-profile Greek women and many Greek men. But, the happy times did not last. The Jews of Thessalonica heard we were in Berea. Some even traveled all the way to Berea to foment an agitation against us among the crowds. But a trend had started—serious Scripture study. We told our Berean friends they were a little unusual with all their excitement over

Scripture. Aneas asked us then, "Is it the normal method of apostles to refer so much to the Jewish Scriptures and read them aloud publicly as part of the teaching?"

"Yes, it is normal," I replied. "Paul did the same in other places. Take Pisidian Antioch. Synagogue leaders there read from the law and then sent a message to Paul asking if he had an exhortation for the people. He did. He demonstrated that time, too, that the old law points to Jesus as Christ. I have watched him do it many times now. He's a master of public dialogue and teaching. You can see that."

Still, let me comment, it's not easy. Even straight public reading can make the reader or listener confused when sentences and words are not divided. It needs a trained reader, and even that person may need to prepare. Paul expected Jews and even Gentile readers to know something of the old law, so, in all the believers' gatherings, someone reads Scriptures aloud. Although Jewish men have learned to read and some women have, often only about one-tenth of Gentiles are literate. That means the churches in the houses do a great deal of reading aloud and explaining the Scriptures. The reading itself becomes a benediction. John wrote once, "Blessed is the one who reads aloud the words of this prophecy, and blessed are those who hear it and take to heart what is written in it."

The focus on religion from a book stems from Jewish thinking and from the very earliest Christians. Right after he rose from the dead, Jesus showed how the old law prepares for the good news. Talking to friends on the road to Emmaus, he asked, "Did not the Messiah have to suffer these things and then enter his glory?" Then he explained the Scriptures about himself. Peter used the same method in his first sermon, saying, "This is what was spoken by the prophet Joel, 'In the last days, God says, I will pour out my Spirit on all people. . . .'" The apostles were always teaching that the death of Christ answers all the old law's foresight.

Well, on with the story of Berea. The same thing happened again there as in so many places—conflict with the Jews, this time fomented by those sent from Thessalonica. Agitation. Opposition. Shouts of, "Who are these people? Why did you let them into our city? We don't want this kind of breach of the peace. Christians, go home."

The new Christ-followers were quick to respond, though. Before anything too big had flared up, elderly Pyrrhus, Sopater's father, called a few together to make a plan. "It's Paul they're uptight about. He's too high-profile," he said.

Noble Leaders in Berea

"Yes," Bion went on. "Luke has Gentile antecedents, and Silas is quieter. Perhaps we can ask them to stay."

Sopater spoke for them all when he said, "We'll have to ask Paul to leave, but only him. That way, we won't lose the chance to keep studying the Scriptures."

"That's a good plan!" exclaimed Agatha. "My husband and I will invite Timothy and Silas to stay with us."

So, then, Sopater, Bion, Pyrrhus, Agatha, her husband Delos, and a few others determined to show their hospitality, even while they had to politely ask Paul to go.

"We're coming down to the coast with you," they said. They each threw a bag across their shoulders for a bottle of water and some bread for the way, and we all escorted Paul down to the sea border and located a ship bound for Athens, 280 miles away to the south. Some went right on with him all the way to Athens.

Timothy and I stayed. It was easy to develop a church or two in homes in Berea. They were so eager. Sopater took the lead locally, and we often met in the large home where he and Pyrrhus lived. I taught those with Jewish background as new people came, showing them where the life and death of Christ is foretold in the old law and now fulfils the longing of their national heart. It strengthened them so much. One of the hardest things was that they had to live among other Jews who believed they had failed their nation by believing and then left the Christian faith. I encouraged Sopater to teach, too. It was his initial apprenticeship. He enabled non-Jews to find boldness to live the Christian life, even if the people around them mocked them for worshiping a God nobody could see.

Besides this, Paul had just prepared his first letter to the Thessalonians, and Timothy and I helped write it. That served as a reminder of themes we should remember to teach. He had taught how to live a pure Christian life and the need to love one another. He taught about the Holy Spirit, about standing firm in the faith, and that they should work for their living and not rely only on the kindness of others. He responded to their questions about what happened when a believer died and about the second coming of Christ. We took up similar topics.

One evening, as Timothy and I reclined over dinner at the home of Agatha and Demos, Sopater came by, too. Timothy, who is curious about

THE PEOPLE PAUL ADMIRED

people's growth as believers, asked, "Sopater, how is it you had an open mind to hear about Christ?"

"That's a good question, Timothy," he replied as he reached to the bowl for more dried figs to munch. "I was a typical Greek boy. You know my father has a shop at the agora, selling lamps, olive oil, flame torches, and braziers. He made sure I started school with a master at age six and learned my *alpha, beta, gamma,* and then reading aloud. I learned my numbers with the abacus counters on rods. The fifteen of us in the school practiced our writing with a wooden sharp-ended stylus on a wooden board covered with layers of wax. We had to be smart at memorizing to repeat poems. I had to learn philosophy, too, and how a state is ruled."

"Were you good at philosophy and politics when you were young, Sopater?"

A grin crossed his face, and he reached for more figs. "Yes. And I was the best debater in the small school. I loved ideas."

"I thought so," quipped Timothy. "I can see that love of debate coming out now, and it was obvious to Paul that you were one to receive extra training. I shall not be surprised if he takes you on a training trip as he has taken me."

"I'm already grateful for all the study and debating he has given me. I'd love to understudy further," he answered. Then he continued, "Father arranged for me to learn the lyre. I picked it up quickly, and used to play a great deal, but, when I was sixteen, I became more interested in athletics. I wanted to be a pentathlon competitor in the Olympic Games, or, if not, the training would be good for getting into the army. I went regularly to the gymnasium for wrestling, long jump, running, throwing discus, and javelin. It was miserably cold in the winter when we had to put aside our chiton and cloak. Some friends did boxing, and the father of one taught him chariot racing, but it was very dangerous.

"Some of the sports were excellent life training. I still take care to avoid cheating, because, if you were caught cheating in sports, you could never compete again.

"Any local games we competed in were, like the big games, a religious event. They sacrificed to Zeus as the king of the gods. I personally was devoted to Ares, the god of war. He is called Mars in Latin. I prayed, but I didn't win in my pentathlon. I kept serving him while I was in the army for five years. 'Ares, exceeding in strength,' I would pray. 'Chariot-rider, golden-helmed, doughty in heart, shield-bearer . . . leader of the

Noble Leaders in Berea

righteous men, sceptered king of manliness . . . Shed down a kindly ray from above upon my life, and strength of war."[1] I wrote poems for him. I sacrificed to him. I learned the myths about him and then found questions in my mind. Manly courage I was happy to learn, but not violence, rage, and adultery. Did I want to follow such a god? I had no peace.

"When I left the army, I went into my father's business. I like bringing light in darkness, and that's what we do selling lamps. However, for myself, I was still searching for a god to fully honor and trust and bring light into my own life.

"Then, you and Paul came to Berea, and a friend told me to come and listen to you and the Jewish people discussing your Scriptures. That appealed to me—a reliable source of information about God. Then, I realized you were describing a God who loved so much he died to make people free from their rotten lives. I listened more. I watched people studying the sacred text. This was what I wanted. Reliability. An honorable God who loves those who serve him. I kept coming, and, soon, I learned to trust this Jesus who is both God and human. He welcomes. Your lives demonstrated willingness to see all people as equal, all able to serve God, nobody depending on priests, a clean way of life. That appealed to me. Feeling free of sin and becoming a friend of a loving God. I held no hesitation."

"What did Pyrrhus, your father, say when you started following a new religion, Sopater?" Timothy asked.

"You know he's elderly now. He did not like it at first. But see how he has come to trust in Christ himself.

"I have rediscovered a talent, too, to use when we hold our first-day-of-the-week gatherings. Remember I learned the lyre? That is most important to me—when I play to worship God the Creator and Jesus the Savior and the Holy Spirit. I get a great deal of pleasure out of playing now. Christians like singing, and that fits with our culture here in Greece—music during religious festivals, at marriage feasts, at funerals, and at banquets. Most men can play an instrument, and some can sing and accompany themselves. Shepherds play pan pipes to their flocks. Men sing the rhythm when they row boats or perform as athletes. I used to sing before my athletics competitions. Soldiers march to drums. Women make music at home. Boys and girls learn instruments and sing

---

1. *Homeric Hymn 8 to Ares.*

and dance. Epics praise famous men, and simple ballads tell folk stories. We are a nation of musicians.

"Have you noticed our Greek instruments? You can see them in the markets, too. We have drums, hand cymbals, castanets, two kinds of lyres with plucked strings, and the *aulos* with its reeds to blow."

We went on talking about music, and then I explained about other Christian groups: "In many cities, Christians can't sing at meetings because they're in antagonistic neighborhoods. They have to avoid drawing attention."

"But it's different in Berea," Agatha observed. "We had lots of singing until those people came from Thessalonica, and, after Paul left, things calmed down anyway. Sometimes, we have all sung beautifully with the instruments and all the voices."

I told how I have noticed that music for churches in homes starts with Jewish-type hymns. Sometimes in a service, a leader sings the phrase and others follow. Psalms are easy when Jewish-background believers know some psalms by heart. When Paul and I sang in the jail in Philippi, psalms came naturally. Singing and praying cheer people through difficult times. James's advice is, if anyone is in trouble, to pray, and if anyone is happy, to sing songs of praise. In Berea, the scene was wide open for music newer than psalms and hymns, for they led on to "songs from the Spirit." These came to believers inspired by the freedom of the new law, some even inspired for a particular occasion.

"I can see you enjoy the singing, Agatha," I commented to the woman who had spoken. "Luke and I have noticed as we travel down the Egnatian Way that women contribute as much as men, for girls in families of substance have often learned singing and instruments."

We did notice women from higher social families becoming prominent in the churches. Lydia's contacts made all the difference on our visit to Philippi, and now we have seen independent women with initiative in two more cities, Thessalonica and Berea—women who are prominent in their Greek societies. Now, we hear that one of the two leading believers in Athens is a woman, Damaris, along with Dionysius. I asked Agatha's opinion: "Do you think it is easier for women with a Greek background to take a leading part in the Christ-following gatherings?"

"I'm sure you're right," she agreed. "Our society is more individualistic and allows more personal development. And our women inherit from their family and retain their property. That's different from the Jewish view that they disappear into their husband's family and do not have assets of their own."

"Hmm. That's true," I commented. "But, let me think. Yes, even some Jewish women are taking a lead among believers. Mary, the mother of Mark, had a fellowship running in her home, and social worker Dorcas in Joppa was a great example of serving in the church. Things are changing for them too."

"Here, in Greek-influenced places, some women are significant on the political scene," Delos explained. "Women's names appear on coins and in inscriptions. They receive honors in some cities, often as benefactors. It is not a large number, perhaps fewer than one in ten, yet they are there. Earlier women were disqualified from public life. Now, some upper-class married women attend civil speeches and religious rituals. Some go shopping and travel."

"I've noticed that in the streets," Timothy put in. "We see some women in commerce with textiles. Some have become believers, like Lydia, who sells cloth and purple dye for cloth. Because women often make sure religion is carried out in the home and family, it perhaps comes across as okay when some are leaders of churches in homes. It does not seem as out of place as it would if women led in a temple. In any case, synagogues do not limit women to one section as the Jewish temple does."

"Tell us about your Jewish mother, Timothy," Sopater inquired.

"That's a good question, Sopater. Paul first met our family in Lystra. My mother, Eunice, was Jewish and became a believer. My father was Greek. That's interesting anyway. Mother made decisions herself, and her marriage was her own choice, not arranged by her parents. Jewish parents do not arrange such marriages. Her Jewish mother was Lois. But Eunice and Lois are both Greek names. Their family had been away from Palestine for some time and absorbed more habits of individualism. They gave me the Greek name Timothy, meaning honoring to God, even though that is a Jewish concept. Later, my mother and grandmother became Christ-believers and introduced me to Christ."

"It's fascinating how much we remain connected to our families and are shaped by our education, isn't it?" Sopater observed, as we wound up for the evening. "You were shaped to take interest in religious life by your mother and grandmother. I was shaped by my schooling and my father. I'm proud to be the son of Pyrrhus. You're proud to be the son of Eunice

THE PEOPLE PAUL ADMIRED

and grandson of Lois. And here we are in Berea, which has become famous for studying the Scriptures, and we're proud of that too."

READER REFLECTION

When you finish reading the chapter seeking to understand the likely house fellowships of Sopater and others in Berea, try writing for yourself a statement of what Bible reading and Bible study mean to you. Or, write a spiritual song that puts into words or music some of your trust in God.

SPEAKER/LISTENER EXPLORATION

If you used the chapter on Sopater and leaders in Berea to speak to a group, discuss and list the influence of Bible teaching in early churches and Christian gatherings. How much difference does that make for Christian groups today? Is the participation of women changing in your context? What significance does music have?

9

Seven Household Hosts in Corinth

Growing the City Church Scene

PEOPLE MENTIONED AS HOUSEHOLDERS OR PROVIDERS OF HOSPITALITY:

- Titius Justus (Acts 18:7)
- Crispus (Acts 18:8, 1 Cor 1:14)
- Gaius (1 Cor 1:14, Rom 16:23)
- Chloe (1 Cor 1:11)
- Priscilla and Aquila (Acts 18:1–3)
- Stephanas (1 Cor 1:16; 16:15, 17)

PRESUMED MEMBERS AND LEADERS MENTIONED AS INDIVIDUALS:

- Fortunatus and Achaicus (1 Cor 16:17)
- Erastus (2 Tim 4:20)
- Apollos (1 Cor 1:12, Acts 18:27—19:1)

WHEN PAUL WROTE TO *the Romans, probably from Corinth, he sent greetings from others in Corinth: Timothy, Lucius, Jason (probably the Jason from Thessalonica), and Sosipater (perhaps a version of Sopater). Tertius, whose name is Latin, wrote the letter; Gaius, Erastus, the city director of public works, and Quartus also sent greetings (Rom 16:21–24).*

To allow ourselves to picture the scene of the churches in Corinth, let us attempt a narrative report such as might come from one of the first church hosts.

THE PEOPLE PAUL ADMIRED

My name is Crispus. I was a leader of the synagogue in Corinth, and I heard about Jews following Jesus of Nazareth before Paul and his friends reached our city. The first time it had anything to do with me came when Paul tramped the fifty miles along the rocky path from Athens and stood up to teach in our synagogue on a Sabbath. We had never heard such teaching, nor in all my life had I seen a religious upheaval like that which happened afterward. First, it affected Jews and our synagogue, then Gentiles, making us devote many hours each week to teaching these new believers , and then causing near riots in the streets of Corinth.

That was only the start. The other leaders and I had even more trouble on our hands later, trying to keep unity among the new believers in Christ and help them grow spiritually. They found so many things to argue for and against that, many times, we were at our wits' end. Paul sent us some long letters to try to improve the situation. Still, a good number of active house churches emerged in our city, even if some started because of divisions. Leaders opened their homes and encouraged others for the sake of Christ. I wish you could join us for worship one First Day of the Week and see the huge level of participation. Our house churches are remarkable.

Let me tell you first about Corinth nearly twenty years after the first Pentecost. We are the result of our geography, with our acropolis hill towering more than 1,880 feet above the city, from where we can even see Athens on a clear day. Our whole commerce depends on proximity to the narrow neck of land that links Achaia with the rest of Greece. Sea traffic passes east/west, and land traffic north/south. We are also the result of our history. We share the heritage of Athens and all southern Greece and its achievements, which made Greek culture known and Greek language used across the Roman Empire. The huge Temple of Apollo, built more than five hundred years ago with enormous fluted columns of single blocks of stone, is still impressive. The theater cut into the hill has room for about 18,000 people, and we still have the architectural splendor of the temple to Aphrodite on the Acrocorinth Hill.

Disaster hit Corinth when Rome conquered our ancestors about two hundred years ago and left the city nearly empty. But, Rome revived us, too, when Julius Caesar refounded the city with freedmen about a hundred years ago. We became a flourishing city again, now with about 80,000 people: Greeks, Romans, Jews, and others. The surrounding walls

Seven Household Hosts in Corinth

are more than six miles long with towers interspersed, enclosing an area two and a half times the size of Athens.

A great deal happens in the agora, the open space surrounded by stone shops and busy with buying and selling. It has a stone-lined water channel and fountain, a judgment seat for magistrates, and a place where speakers make public addresses. Because we are so near to major ports, people come and go—sailors, dockyard workers, traders, and government officials. That has repercussions, too, for their uninhibited behavior gives our city a reputation for immorality and prostitution, including religious prostitution at temples. They say there are a thousand male and female prostitutes at the Temple of Aphrodite on the Acropolis.

In contrast, our Jewish community keeps its own higher standards and holds regular services in the synagogue where Sosthenes and I were the leaders. We also had good working relationships with some non-Jews who worshiped the one true God—people like the Roman man Titius Justus who lived next to the synagogue.

The ports are important. On the west is Lechaeum and on the east Cenchrea and Schoenus. Shipmasters have a choice for their cargo: 3.5 miles across the isthmus, dragging it on rollers, or traveling 200 miles around the peninsula, and that is not advisable during the winter. Laborers haul smaller ships cross the isthmus on logs, and larger ships often transfer their cargo, so there are many jobs available at the ports. Workers can earn, and there is little serious poverty.

We have two notable products from Corinth. Farmers nearby grow linen-flax and process it for weaving linen cloth and rope. This is unusual, as most people north of the Great Sea wear wool. In addition, near Corinth, rural people breed horses and mules. Most often in our athletic contests, Corinthians win the equestrian events.

About the time Paul first visited us, the city held Isthmian Games[1] in honor of Poseidon, god of the sea. Corinthians competed in front of large crowds against rivals from other parts of Macedonia, Achaia, and the Aegean islands in athletics, horse riding, and music, with categories for men, youths, and boys. People loved the spectacle of footraces, races in armor, throwing discus and javelin, two-horse chariot races, and the hand-fighting combination of boxing and wrestling. However, the games did lose some of their sparkle, for the top-rate professionals who trained

---

1. This was about AD 51.

THE PEOPLE PAUL ADMIRED

hard and kept a strict diet were infiltrated by quacks and hawkers. Some were making money as fortune-tellers.

Religiously, the city is cosmopolitan, like its people. Because of Rome's influence, there are shrines to Julius Caesar, to Octavia, and to the goddess Roma as part of the cult planned to hold the empire together. Many people already worshiped Greek gods, and they added Astarte of the Phoenicians as well, worshiping her as Aphrodite.

As in many other cities, everyone must show their loyalty to the city and to Rome by worshipping at the shrines. Nearly all society becomes caught up in this ruler cult, and social climbers donate the money, food, wine, and organization for feasts at temples or for animal sacrifices at athletic games or theaters in the name of Caesar, Roma, or another god. If Greek believers in Christ stay away, people think them antisocial, or even traitors, and that can mean trouble.

We Jews were exempt from emperor worship, however, since the Romans recognized we would never comply, and we were a significant minority making up nearly one-fifth of the city. But, we had our own problems later with contention from overzealous Jews that led to the riot around Paul when Gallio ruled as proconsul. Praise God, Gallio told us Jews to settle it among ourselves and refused to be part of the attack.

When Paul arrived, he stayed with Jewish Aquila and his wife Priscilla, who had recently migrated from Rome because Claudius Caesar evicted all Jews. They had already heard of Christ and believed in him. Since this couple worked as makers of tents, they set up a business in Corinth, and Paul worked with them during the week, for he had done his apprenticeship earlier in tent-making and preferred to earn his way.

Paul preached in our synagogue. Let me ask you to think what this would mean. He told us Jews, "The Messiah has come, and our people in Jerusalem missed the point. They persuaded the Romans to execute the Messiah." Imagine the stir.

"What is this nonsense?" they said. "Who is this?" "But they say he's a Pharisee. Is that true?" "I can't believe it. A Pharisee would never say that." "The Messiah killed on a Roman cross! I never heard such a thing!"

For a few Sabbaths, they listened, but soon, they either liked or loathed the teaching. Stephanas's family believed first. It was an immense shock to my family and me when he and his household were baptized. They were very bold, but being baptized was like a red rag to a bull in the view of other Jews, and they came down heavy on us. What an uproar!

Seven Household Hosts in Corinth

"Shame on you! Call yourself a Jew? God's curse be on you for teaching such heresy! Get out of this place, or we'll make you. See the truncheon I carry? It loves work. It will make short work of you."

Paul kept his cool, shook out his clothes in protest, and explained, "Your blood be on your own heads. I am innocent of it. From now on, I will go to the Gentiles."

This started the meetings in houses. Titius Justus invited Paul, Silas, and Timothy to teach in his home. We were amazed again. A Latin-speaking Roman had welcomed Paul, a Pharisee, to teach next door to the synagogue.

But now, I had to make a decision. The synagogue had divided, and my household and I had to decide whose side we were on. Some thought the teaching that Jesus was the Christ was heresy, and some accepted it as the power of God. Jews wanted signs, and Greeks wanted wisdom. I turned over in my mind the whole scene: "I have listened to Paul and the others. Their version of recent history? It makes sense. There are indeed many pointers in the old law that the Messiah will come in humility, not as a conquering king. God loves, but also sets standards. I believe in Jesus as the Messiah. Someone had to take the punishment for human sin."

I talked with my wife, Helena. "What do you think, Helena? Do you think Jesus is really the Messiah? Will you stick with me if I follow Jesus?" Praise God, she stayed with me. Some of the people in our household had heard the teaching, and we passed it on to others. Some of them believed, too, so we followed the household of Stephanas and requested baptism—and Paul baptized us.

That caused more disturbance and outright animosity. Even Paul and his friends were afraid. God gave them a vision that helped them and us: "Do not be afraid; keep on speaking; do not be silent. For I am with you, and no one is going to attack and harass you, because I have many people in this city." That fortified our spirits. Knowing that more people would believe gave us inner staying power and courage to proclaim the message, even if we felt afraid.

Most people who turned to follow Christ were not upper class. Paul commented later, "Not many of you were influential; not many were of noble birth. But God chose the foolish things of the world to shame the wise." As you can guess, some people's thinking did a complete reversal. Jews already admiring high ethical standards learned that Messiah had come, had died and risen, and had taught a new kind of ethics for a new kingdom that rested on God's love, not only on punishment. But, our Jewish people are convinced they are right. They resist other religions vociferously or accept martyrdom for the faith. For us to change our minds on this conviction was earth-shattering. The full anger of extended families descended on new believers. Greek and Roman religious communities were tight, but not as tight as Jewish ones. They, too, anxiously put pressure on new believers to appear loyal to the city and to the Roman Empire, for they knew they would face persecution if they did not comply.

Strategically, Paul, and then also Silas and Timothy, who came across from Berea, taught in the home of Titius Justus. They gave us who attended grounding in the new beliefs so we could teach more people, especially the great majority who could not read, in the gatherings that grew up as a result in homes around the city. The larger Greek houses had open courtyards at the center or side with a row of columns. Roman houses, only slightly different, had an entryway to a courtyard and a room with an opening in the roof for light and to collect rain in a small tank in the floor. Most often, the believing brothers and sisters met in the dining room. The custom was that only nine people could dine there reclining on couches, yet a room could fit twenty to thirty people when they sat on rush mats on the floor, so most did that.

At first, some opposition came from other Jews, but householders could use their freedom to choose what they did in their own homes, opening to the non-Jews who crowded in. I can tell you of at least six homes in Rome and another fellowship over at Cenchrea Port where Phoebe was a minister.

The owner of the first household, Titius Justus, may have found it easier to avoid the sneers of relations and neighbors since he was Roman, and Jews and local Greeks were more agitated here about the new teaching. He could most easily offer his home and encourage the church gatherings. The people in the second household, that of Stephanas, were bold and devout. Anybody could go to the gathering in their house.

My home became a meeting place after we received baptism. That was natural, as I was already a leader and well educated, though no longer a teacher in the synagogue, for we had made our decision and moved out in the middle of all the trouble. Did I say "natural"? That is only half the story. Yes, as a leader, I wanted to encourage others to believe that Jesus was the Messiah, but it was not natural to bring on ourselves the storm of fury and scorn from people I had known all my life—my own family,

Seven Household Hosts in Corinth

uncles, cousin-brothers I had grown up with, and, of course, my wife's family. It was a tense time. Who knew whether an angry member of our own community would hire a thug to beat up me or one of my children on the street? Who knew whether someone would poison the mind of one of my servants, or poison our food, or accidentally on purpose empty filthy buckets from their parapets on us as we went past? Swiftly, there came a problem with my son's schooling. He had attended class at the synagogue, but then, not surprisingly, they would not let him continue because I had left the synagogue. I had to employ a tutor.

As the leader in the synagogue, I had not been a priest. I was a lay leader and had a business, but that was disrupted, too. Jewish customers avoided me like the plague. Suddenly, there was almost no income, and I had to get out into the marketplace and make more business contacts.

My wife and I talked it all through with the staff and the older children. It was one thing to believe in Jesus as the Messiah, but it was another to face all these dislocations. Was that enough to cope with? Or would we also invite people to our house for Jesus-as-Messiah gatherings? Having people coming to the house would be observed and would draw more attention, opening the whole household to scorn, or even risk. Were they willing to do it? I wanted to, and they said yes, too. We opened our home and made many people welcome. We were the third household.

Chloe, a woman of substance, had believers and seekers coming to her home. I think she briefed her staff rather carefully on getting to know everyone and checking out security issues before they entered. Not being Jewish gave her some advantages.

Gaius, a Roman, became extremely hospitable with his large house. Paul wrote about him later that the whole church enjoys his hospitality. We had occasional gatherings of all the house groups there.

The sixth household was that of the business couple, Priscilla and Aquila, who housed live-in workers, clients, and traders. Since they were newcomers with fewer contacts and no relatives in the city, being Christ-followers did not bring so much disparagement and ridicule on their heads. While Paul worked with them and resided at their *familia*, many people treated their house as a haven of safety where they could go to learn the new teaching. Aquila and Priscilla impressed Paul with how brilliantly they used their business and home premises for the gospel.

One day, when Helena and I were over at the home of Gaius, our conversation turned to how different our setup is from most structures in society. I commented, "We followers of the Way are peculiar."

"What do you mean?" Gaius asked.

"We do not have priests or a single leader of a church group or city group. When Paul wrote to our churches in Corinth, even when he wanted to correct something wrong, he wrote to all the members of the churches, asking them to put it right. He assumed we were a team of leaders and never picked out an individual as the sole leader."

"I notice that too," Helena added. "Even for ceremonies like baptism and the memory supper, individuals are not celebrants like priests. Paul expected team leadership of elders and deacons. Some people are most surprised. They like much more the idea of official positions."

"Yes, yet, Jesus had already taught the concept of not making some people higher than others, hadn't he?" I reminded. "He described how people love to be the first in position and categorically told the disciples things must not be like that with them. It is hard for some of us to change, but changing gives longer-term answers with a focus on functioning well rather than on holding office regardless of ability or performance."

"That must have been Paul's policy," Gaius agreed. "He taught here in Corinth for eighteen months and then moved on to Ephesus, and then onward, for he had coached us to function without him. It was up to us to keep up the task as teachers and leaders. What did we need to do for that? We taught Jews through the Jewish Scriptures, showing them where Christ was foretold and how Jesus fulfilled the prophecies of the Messiah who would come. With Romans and Greeks and people from the islands, we taught that luck and spells, fortunetelling, and offerings of food and wine to gods have nothing to do with how a loving, all-seeing God controls the world. We said they could throw out their good-luck charms and spells, and they would never need a magician or fortune-teller again. We taught them how to love and trust a God who answers prayer and who heals when believers lay on hands, anoint with oil, and pray. Then, we taught the new ethic: life in relationship with the Spirit of Jesus means an end to idol worship and an end to feuds, fights, and squabbles so that all can live together like brothers and sisters."

"But we have not always succeeded, have we?" I had to admit.

"Yes, I wish it were not like that. Our people are human, still tainted with human weakness and wrong choices. Still, there was some progress. We did persuade people we are responsible to God for each other in some way and that we are a caring community where we look after one another when someone is ill or in trouble and help with basic needs for food and shelter."

Helena had some positives to mention: "Here in Corinth, people have grown to love our gatherings. We enjoy the prayers, psalms, spiritual songs, prophecies, and tongues within our protocol, as well as healings, wide participation, breaking of bread, and the teaching of those who have wonderful good news to tell."

Helena was right, of course. However, I regret to say that quarrels did spring up among us. At one stage, after Paul went to Ephesus and Priscilla and Aquila had given Apollos some teaching there, Apollos himself came here and taught. He debated with great skill, vigorously refuting the Jews in public, proving from the Scriptures that Jesus was the Messiah. But he impressed the believers so much that they took sides, forming fan clubs, you could say. Some said they belonged to Paul's fan club, some to those of Apollos or Peter or Christ.

The division gave us big headaches. Eventually, some folk from Chloe's household went traveling, met Paul, and told him about the cliques forming. He dipped his pen in the ink and told everybody smartly that he would have none of this—no fan club for him or anybody else. "Is Christ divided?" he wrote. "Was Paul crucified for you? Were you baptized in the name of Paul?" "What, after all, is Apollos? And what is Paul? Only servants, through whom you believe. . . . We are God's coworkers." We were pleased he did that. He did not want anyone to put him or anybody else on a pedestal. He made it clear too that, if there were arguments, people in the house churches must not turn them into lawsuits and go to nonbelieving judges, but ask believers to hear their views.

Let me also tell some good points about our fellowships. The new meaning of "family" for us has joined us together. We have all these homes open to people of different races and different economic levels, Jew or Gentile, slave or free. We welcome those who already follow Jesus and those who want to learn. We welcome different gifts and know what Paul meant when he wrote of unity and gifting. He said, "The eye cannot say to the hand, 'I don't need you!' and the head cannot say to the feet, 'I don't need you!'" When members face jibes from family, exclusion from the synagogue, ostracism for not joining idol worship, or serious persecution, they know they can turn to their new family where each will be treated as an important part of the body.

Because of the kind of city Corinth is, we needed extra teaching about the body in two different ways: the sacredness of the human body, and how believers are like the body of Christ. Temples to all kinds of gods are big in the thinking of people in Corinth, and their immorality affects the whole of society. We household leaders often had to back up the teaching Paul gave when he said, "Don't you know that you yourselves are God's temple and that God's Spirit dwells in your midst?" He rebuked some members for sexual immorality when we had not been able to correct them adequately: "Do you not know that your bodies are members of Christ himself? Shall I then take the members of Christ and unite them with a prostitute? Never!" This teaching hit right between the eyes for our context. Our society compromises so much on sex life. Paul knew what we and others need: "Flee sexual immorality. All other sins people commit are outside their bodies, but those who sin sexually sin against their own bodies. . . . You were bought with a price. Therefore, honor God with your bodies."

The other teaching about the body is entirely different. Paul pictured the church as having different parts with different abilities like a human body. Church life is about acting together with love for each other as much as a body acts intrinsically to the advantage of each member. Church is nothing if its members are not all out in favor of each other with each one acting for the good of the whole. It is unity in diversity. Paul told us to be united: "Just as a body, though one, has many parts, but all its many parts form one body—whether Jews or Gentiles, slave or free."

In our house churches, we feel related to one another. Paul told us we are the body of Christ. It is part of our self-definition that we will not allow class or racial divisions, nor will we envy each other's gifts. All gifts are valuable. All are needed, and Paul encouraged everyone that each could become a prophet. Before the teaching of Christ reached us, the greatest honor fell on those who were free, male, Roman citizens. Now slaves, females, Greeks, Jews, and other races and classes are counted in as equals, and all can contribute in our church.

That is visible when we gather. Some sing, some pray, some tell recent news, some teach or give an interpretation that God has given them. Some prophesy, some speak in tongues, and some interpret the tongues. It is all valuable and builds the spiritual strength of the believers. Sometimes, two or three prophesy one after another because God has given them the gift and something to say.

We are learning yet, but we have come a long way. There is still a great deal about our churches that I have not mentioned, but let me finish with this: Paul wrote to us one of his most well-known sayings, and we take it as a challenge to keep discovering the meaning of love through the Spirit of God. He said, "If I have a faith that can remove mountains, but do not have love, I am nothing. . . . Love is patient, love is kind. . . . It always protects, always trusts, always hopes, and always perseveres."

READER REFLECTION

When you finish reading the chapter on Crispus and the other leaders in Corinth, pause to contemplate the inherent dynamics of leaders, teams, and people in their recognition of the contributions from many. Where do you fit at this point in your life? Where does God want you to be next?

SPEAKER/LISTENER EXPLORATION

If you used the chapter on Crispus and the other leaders in Corinth to speak to a group, make a list of things the Christians of Corinth were learning, and a second list of what they had so far learned under their several leaders. Where does love belong in each list?

10

Minister Phoebe in Cenchrea

The Protector of Many

MAIN SCRIPTURE SOURCE: Romans 16:1–2, 21–24

ALTHOUGH PAUL MENTIONS HER *only briefly in Romans 16, Phoebe is worthy of note. She is the only person cited in the New Testament with a named leadership task deacon/servant/minister in a named church outside of Jerusalem. The respect of Paul and other leaders for her and the crucible of her everyday life and decisions in a house church must have shaped Phoebe for appropriate actions as a woman leader. Some say that, in Palestine, women held an honored position as mothers in society, and others say that they were passive, voiceless, and barely allowed outside the house. Some comment that women in the Greco-Roman world led restricted lives mostly inside four walls. Others note they could inherit from their families and manage finances, a few had spoken in the Senate and law court, some swayed politics and policy in their cities through the people they knew, and some were influential as public donors and patrons. Both stances on the scene may be true. There were vast differences in women's lives, and the differences lay with families, cultures, and especially the range of status in society.*

Timothy was with Paul when he wrote of Phoebe. Let us conjecture his account of something of her life.

One springtime about five years after our first visit to Corinth, our patron, Phoebe, sent a message over to Paul where he and I and his other

Minister Phoebe in Cenchrea

assistants Lucius, Jason, and Sosipater were staying in roomy accommodations in the household of Gaius. Phoebe believed in Christ during Paul's first eighteen months of teaching in Corinth. A Gentile woman, she ministered in the church in Cenchrea, the seaport on the eastern side of the isthmus. (Our attention focused on Cenchrea again some months later when, before sailing for Jerusalem, Paul had a haircut there because of a vow he had taken.)

Phoebe asked Paul to attend a service in her church on Sunday, giving teaching. Paul accepted, and Jason and I walked the five miles over with him while our friends taught in other house churches in Corinth. Phoebe and Heliodoros entertained us with a delicious lunch afterward with grapes, olives, fresh bread, cucumbers in vinegar dressing, and tasty fresh-caught sea fish. Heliodoros is often away from home to look after his family land and horse-breeding business. He rears horses for the army, and some of his horses did well at the last Isthmus Games.

Phoebe had a personal request: "I'm planning a trip to Rome for my family's bronze business," she said. "Would you introduce me to the believers in Rome by writing a commendation?"

Paul did not hesitate. "Of course I'll do that," he said. And then he thought further. "When are you leaving?"

"In about four weeks, Paul. I hope to find ships going and coming so I can make the voyage and return before the winds of returning winter. With the six hundred miles each way between Corinth and Rome, I'll be traveling for eight weeks. I'll take my steward, Atticus, with me. That way, I'll have some assistance and protection. Almost nobody travels alone, especially not a woman."

"Well, I've got a further idea. Would you be able to take a major letter to the friends in Rome for me? I would start work on it this week and bring it over to you when it is all written. I want to explain to them that I am most keen to visit Rome and get to know them better and contribute to the teaching there. However, I have to make a visit to Jerusalem first with the collection I have arranged for the friends there."

"Certainly, I would be most happy to carry a letter."

"That's great. Are you seeking more trading contacts? It's always like that, isn't it? The more networks the better. Perhaps you'll be busy with product samples in the next while."

THE PEOPLE PAUL ADMIRED

"Definitely. My father wants me to take a few valuable bronze vases and our specialty sundials for new contacts there. It will be two or three wooden barrels, I guess. Atticus will help with that."

"My package will be light, but vulnerable in a way," Paul explained. "It must not get water near it. Hmm. It will be a busy four weeks. I'll ask Tertius if he could write for me. He is experienced at persevering with rough papyrus and at taking dictation. That will leave me free to think carefully while he writes."

We talked on for a while. None of us had visited Rome, but we had heard enough about hazards on the way. Wise captains decline to put to sea until the weather is fine, and providing food and water for all the rowers takes enormous logistical planning.

Then, Paul offered another idea. "I think I should call you patron in the letter, Phoebe. We need to give credit where credit is due, and you have been a patron to many people, including me."

"I like that idea, Paul," Jason commented. "Whenever anyone says *patron*, people automatically think of a man, someone who is a leader in the agora, in the city council, or in donating funds for the Isthmus Games or a statue. But, women do it too."

"Yes, that is part of my thinking. Patronage is a big part of how society works. Decisions do lie often with whom you know and whom you have been introduced to. Here on the isthmus, patronage helped me and my team enormously. First, there was acceptance by the synagogue leaders because of my identity as a Pharisee. Then, when I stayed in the home of Priscilla and Aquila, when they were still here, they were my patrons for accommodation, work, and introductions. You did that for me in Thessalonica, too, Jason, when you invited us to your home. It grew to be even more significant when the authorities made you sign that paper taking responsibility that there would be no more risks to public peace."

"Yes, in that context, I was the patron who helped you. Here, when I am the assistant preacher and you are the leader, you are the patron and I am the benefactor."

"Agreed. In a slightly different way, every person who lives in a household has the household head as his or her patron. In Philippi, Lydia was a patron for us. Perhaps also we can be grateful that she, as our patron there, organized the financial donations she sent to us when we were in Thessalonica."

I added a comment here. "Patronage among Christians is a blessing, isn't it? Look how Phoebe has assisted us here. With her high connections, she put in a word with city leaders that we were respectable travelling teachers. That gave us the freedom to stay in the city without being hassled by the authorities. And, remember, if ever there were accusations of disrupting the peace, Phoebe spoke to the magistrate and got the matter tidied up before it became a big issue."

"And think of the times she has arranged for Christians to stay at her household," Jason commented. "That is such a boon, keeping us from having to go to seedy public inns inhabited by thieves, prostitutes, and bedbugs."

Paul spoke again. "Do you remember when I took a trip along the coast to Athens? Phoebe sent Atticus along with me as bodyguard, and gave the money for our food as well."

"I think that, even for slaves, the patronage system gives benefits," Phoebe commented. "Many do not seek freedom, as they have no assets with which to manage on their own and prefer to stay with a kindly patron. However, for slaves and prostitutes, the patronage system can be used wrongly, and then it abuses people."

"Yes, I've seen that," observed Paul. "It can be good or bad. But I think of artists and musicians. They need a patron to commission paintings or statues or invite them for music or drama on public occasions. They cannot take the time to excel in their skills unless someone provides for their living. Some large households have a resident priest in a similar way."

"You are also right when you say that being a patron can apply to women as easily as men, depending on their financial circumstances," Phoebe continued. "I've thought about Jewish women, too, like Mary mother of Mark welcoming a prayer meeting in her home. Besides, Joanna wife of Chuza, Susannah, and Mary Magdalene supported Jesus and the disciples from their own finances. They, too, were benefactors—patrons of a kind."

"Now you, Phoebe, have asked Paul to be patron to you in a different way," Jason went on. "When he gives you an introduction to Christians you will meet in Rome, it's as if he is the patron rather than you."

"I like it, don't you?" she smiled. "There are so many variations on the theme of being a patron."

THE PEOPLE PAUL ADMIRED

Before we left that day, Phoebe took us out to see the bronze works behind her home. Bronze articles are among the main exports of Corinth. Phoebe's father, still alive but elderly, had passed over most of the business operation to her. Different from the Jewish system, people see married Greek and Roman women as continuing as members of their birth family, and their dowry is theirs, not their husband's. We saw the cauldron ready for the copper from Cyprus and the precious supplies of tin from Anatolia to be mixed in to make the strong metal alloy. To the side lay stacks of wood to fire the smelter. Vast tracts of forest in Greece have disappeared because of the smelting of ore. An outbuilding held the valuable tools: molds, hammers, anvils, and knives. Workers' lodges formed an arc on the northern side. Some families enjoyed the sun's warmth in the south-facing sunny yard. They get a holiday on Sunday because Phoebe is a Christian. Most day-workers in the city do not get a day off.

I voiced my curiosity about musical instruments: "Do you make some of the famous Corinthian gongs and cymbals at this yard, Phoebe? I recall you mentioned them, Brother Paul, in your first letter to the believers in Corinth."

"Yes, we have them, too," Phoebe smiled, as she pointed. "You young people are always thinking about music. Look over in the storeroom on the right." I wandered over while the others talked. I took a bar and struck a cymbal hanging on a wall. "Bo-o-o-o-o-ng," it echoed out resonantly. Lucky Phoebe with all those instruments.

Paul sounded full of his new project as we walked nearly two hours home to Gaius's house. "I already know so many people in Rome whom I have met in other places. I'm keen to contact them. There are others I have heard of from travelers to places like Ephesus and here. Some are Jewish and some Gentile."

"There's been so much discussion on whether it is an advantage to be Jewish. Will you include that?" I asked.

"Certainly, that must go in. God's love reaches out to both Jews and Gentiles. I shall be praying for God to guide me about what to include. I can already see we need a big section on being dead to sin and alive to Christ. Life in the Spirit. I'll start making notes. Will you go over to Tertius's house tomorrow morning, Timothy? Ask him to come and discuss this. I'll give you some coins to purchase papyrus sheets and pens, too."

"Yes, I'll do that. And I'll mix the soot, gum, and oil for ink."

Of course, Tertius agreed, and the task soon began, but there was much trouble finding good quality papyrus. It comes from reeds on the River Nile in Egypt and has to be imported. The first lot I bought was terribly rough. Every time Tertius dipped his pen, he had to scratch and double-stroke on the letters. He dipped again after four or five letters and tried to persuade the ink to hold on to the surface. Paul prayed earnestly each day before he started. He laid out his writing plan and even then sometimes felt prompted to shift his thinking while he dictated. It takes only 140 words to cover each ten-inch sheet, and that takes two hours.

I purchased light pumice stone to rub the papyrus and try to make it smoother. I kept a sharp knife to keep up the supply of sharpened split reeds. I mixed more ink. I kept a sponge to erase mistakes and to blot the reed when it took too much ink. Sometimes, I checked the agora shops for better papyrus. I looked over the manuscript Tertius was preparing with all its upper-case letters and all the words run together. It would still be quite hard to read. I counted the days. Time was running out. Paul sent me over to Phoebe again.

"Have you found a ship that's going to Rome, Phoebe?"

"Yes, we talked to the captain. It's all fixed for next Monday, leaving from Lechaeum Port on the west of the isthmus."

"Next Monday! My word, Paul and Tertius will have to hurry. Will it be okay in leather pouches? It's far too big to fold. It will be rolls of papyrus. Leather parchment is too expensive for a large manuscript."

"Yes. Here's another thought. Could you prepare a parchment inner pocket as well as the outer carrying case? These will be valuable documents, and I don't want them splashed by the oars or damaged by wild sea weather."

"That's an excellent plan," I agreed, and hurried off to a leather worker to make more arrangements.

On the last day of writing, we kept working through the afternoon so we would finish the last section with all its greetings.

"Who wants to send their greetings to the friends in Rome?" Paul called as several of the household sopped their flatbread in the kitchen before the day's work.

"Count me in," responded Lucius. Jason and Sosipater joined in.

Of course, I said, "Yes, send my greetings," and Tertius got his chance because he was doing the writing.

THE PEOPLE PAUL ADMIRED

Gaius said, "Please send my best wishes, and that goes for the whole fellowship that meets here." Later, while we reclined after dinner, nibbling raisins from last year's harvest, we got into a discussion. Gaius and Paul were looking over the manuscript.

"You called Phoebe a deacon as well as a patron, Paul. I know you think a woman can do that task, but it has never been our custom. I see women like Priscilla, Chloe, and Phoebe doing work that was never seen before among Jewish, Greek, or Roman women."

"Interesting change, isn't it," Paul responded. "There are good reasons for it. I guess we all feel fine about women praying in our fellowships, as I mentioned in my first letter, and even leading and hosting prayer, as you will have heard Mary the mother of John Mark did early on with a meeting in her home."

"Yes, those are fine in my thinking. I notice you include women prophesying in that letter too, where you wrote about appropriate head coverings."

"Mmm. I'm serious about that. I took care not to stipulate men or women prophesying when I wrote several times in that letter that we ought all to desire the greatest gifts, and especially to prophesy. To me, prophecy is next after being an apostle. A prophet receives a message from God and passes it on to his people. We know God gave women the gift of prophecy in years past and showed Peter at Pentecost that what was happening fulfilled the long hope that sons and daughters, young men, and old people would receive prophecies, dreams, and visions. God would pour out his Spirit on men and women, and they would prophesy. Women are priests, too. Earlier, as a Pharisee, I thought all priests were men, but I've changed. What do you see as a priest's task?"

"A priest mediates between people and God."

"And who is now the one mediator between people and God?"

"That is Jesus Christ, of course. I see what you mean. We do not need human priests now. We can all pray directly to Christ."

"Yes, we have learned that, haven't we? We are all priests. So your wife Isis can pray to God through Christ as much as you can. She is a priest."

"Yes, but it's a big change. It seems okay for women you have written greetings to in Rome, and for Priscilla and Chloe, and Phoebe. I admire them. But is Isis my equal now?"

"I like to say, 'Submit one to one another.' You do this together."

Minister Phoebe in Cenchrea

"But, Brother Paul, you said in your commendation section that Phoebe ministers in the church in Cenchrea. That is more than a host."

"Yes, though it follows from host. A minister, *diakonos*, is a servant in the sense of serving Christ and the church, but you know how this can be a highly responsible position. A servant can be an official in charge of the emperor's work, and King Solomon had servants and officials supervising work. The first deacons or ministers in our movement served at tables, but even then, Philip and Stephen were also preachers and teachers. I call myself a servant of Christ, the same word I use for Phoebe. I used it in the first letter, too: 'Servants of Christ entrusted with the mysteries God has revealed.' It's a responsible trust, and a minister/deacon must prove faithful in serving and in teaching. That applies to Phoebe as to all of us."

"Then how does a deacon serve, Paul?"

"Some things are obvious. Leading prayer, acting as a shepherd to guide the believers, attending to the spiritual needs of people. I summarize it this way in my instructions to deacons: 'Devote yourself to the public reading of Scripture, to preaching and to teaching. Take part responsibly in decisions. Do not neglect your gift, which was given you. . . . Watch your life and doctrine closely. Persevere in them, because, if you do, you will save both yourself and your hearers.'"

"Thanks. That clarifies many things. I noticed what you said about the women in Rome to whom you sent greetings, too. The importance you give them is the same as that to men. You call men 'fellow prisoners, fellow workers, hard workers who risked their necks, people who labored by your side in the gospel.' You described both women and men as 'fellow prisoners, fellow workers, hard workers who risked their necks for you and labored side by side with you in the gospel.'"

"That was quick. Yes, I do that because it was what Jesus did. Peter can remember, and Luke discovered it when he did his research for writing. They tell me how Jesus treated women with great respect, not only as mothers, but also as fellow followers of God. Our Lord Jesus thought they were worthy of his time, conversation, healing, and teaching. That attitude was so different from the actions of my fellow Pharisees. He broke society's taboos about not touching women or talking with them. He discussed theology with the woman at the well, with Mary in her home, and with Martha over death and resurrection. He did not define women only as mothers to feel proud of sons, but pointed to the greater need to serve God."

THE PEOPLE PAUL ADMIRED

Luke had been sitting by listening to the long discussion. Now, he added an important point. "I have noticed another thing. God's planning ignored the Jewish view that a woman's voice does not count in a law court. You would think a vital legal matter like the fact that Jesus was alive and had conquered sin and death should come from the most reliable witnesses, meaning men. Yet, somehow, God planned that women gave the first witness that he had risen. God must think their witness worthy of trust. It was the biggest news of all time, and God viewed a woman's voice as having authority!"

"All right," Gaius interjected. "Please don't see me as arguing, but help me understand, Paul. Why did you put restrictions on women in your first letter to our churches here? Words about not talking in the church gathering."

"Oh, Gaius, you know what illiterate people are like—rarely having learned to sit still and receive instruction. The women don't get schooling, and they are often the ones who chat. They need to take care not to interrupt. Just a few sentences before that, I said that those who spoke in tongues should be quiet, too. That's for a circumstance—not permanent."

"Oh, I see. Thanks for explaining that."

I took the chance to ask the next question. "Paul, do you think that society accepts women acting just the same as men?"

"Good question," he replied, and I felt pleased I had asked the right thing. "No, I don't. It is a little different outside our fellowships. When women or men follow Christ, they automatically have to walk a careful path between new ways and expected cultural norms. You know how most people divide life into private and public spheres, and place men in the public sphere and women in the private? They say, 'A woman's place is in the home.' So, usually, upper-class women have kept out of public view, or, if present, keep silent in marketplaces, halls, and councils. It's different for poorer women, who carry water, work in fields, gather firewood, and tend sheep and goats. They have little choice, and their society does not require them to stay in the house.

"You know how this ties social standing to modesty, and honor and shame to dress codes? People think a woman is shamed if she does not keep the dress code of her social class, so that impinges on what people think of Christians. We must not let people gossip and discredit Christ for the wrong reasons. That's why I tell women to wear a head covering where their society requires it, even if they take a lead in our churches."

Paul's explanation helped me. Now Gaius and Luke were getting up, so, before we separated, I offered my suggestion for Monday.

"I've got an idea, friends. This letter has been a huge effort, and it is full of some of Paul's deepest teaching. Phoebe is a remarkable lady taking it to Rome. What do you say we all go to an eating-place in Lechaeum for breakfast on Monday morning? We can celebrate all the hard work and pray for Phoebe before she boards ship."

"Great idea," Gaius thumped the couch he was reclining on. "We'll do it."

So, Monday morning found us in Alexio's eatery, tucking in to oven-bread with olives and goat cheese, pan-bread with mint and radish chutney, and fresh grape juice. Around the table were Gaius and Isis, Jason, Lucius, Tertius, Paul and me, Atticus, Phoebe, and Heliodoros.

Gaius spoke first: "I am thankful to God you are such a strong person, Phoebe. You live in an environment that is not fully safe, among people who at times actively oppose your Christian faith. You take on more risk as you travel. We pray safety for you as you set off now."

Tertius voiced his thoughts, influenced by the words he took in dictation. "You are a sister in Christ, a minister of the gospel, and the patron of many of us. We admire you. May God bless you and guide you on this journey."

"We are all counting on you, Phoebe," Paul urged. "You carry my biggest epistle to date. Yet, we know you have already carried out a ministry in your own church and will honorably represent your church to the churches in Rome. What do you think of this wife of yours, Heliodoros?"

Heliodoros grinned. "She's amazing. What man wants to take on the hazards of travel by ship with the danger of storms and pirates, and then by land, with the bad weather, bandits, and unscrupulous innkeepers? Yet, this wife of mine goes off with only her steward to help her in the task. When they land, she will hike on foot from Puteoli to Rome. She's strong physically, mentally, and spiritually. But please pray for her as well, Paul. She needs God's help and help from the friends in Rome."

Gaius prayed then. He thanked God for all the long task of writing that Paul and Tertius had completed. Then, Paul beseeched God to protect our friend and patron Phoebe. And God did. The letter reached Rome safely and was read and treasured by the recipients it addressed so warmly.

THE PEOPLE PAUL ADMIRED

READER REFLECTION

When you finish reading the chapter on Phoebe, consider the biblical meaning of the three words used of Phoebe: sister, deacon, and patron. Does culture matter for you where *you* are in place and time? Has culture changed since your parents' time? Have your views on women in leadership changed? List the ways you support your views from the New Testament.

SPEAKER/LISTENER EXPLORATION

If you used the chapter on Phoebe to speak to a group, ask them to discuss how the three words used of Phoebe—sister, deacon, and patron—worked out on the ground. What is the reality of these three words in relation to women leaders in the present day?

11

The Couple Ministry of Priscilla and Aquila in Ephesus

Quintessential House Church Leaders

SCRIPTURE SOURCES:
PRISCILLA AND AQUILA IN CORINTH: Acts 18:1–3
PRISCILLA AND AQUILA IN EPHESUS: Acts 18:18–19, 24–26;
later, 1 Corinthians 16:19, later again, 2 Timothy 4:19
PRISCILLA AND AQUILA IN ROME: Romans 16:3–4

MANY OTHER CHRISTIAN VISITORS and residents in Ephesus for shorter or longer spells are named: Apollos, Timothy and Erastus, Tychicus, Onesiphorus, Gaius, and Aristarchus. Three visitors from Corinth refreshed Paul's spirit when he visited Ephesus.1 Traditionally, John the apostle lived here for many years.

When Emperor Claudius expelled Jews from Rome, it was AD 49, and Priscilla and Aquila met Paul in Corinth in about AD 51. They were probably already followers of Christ, for Luke does not ascribe their conversion to contact with Paul. Scholars give later approximate dates as follows:

- *Aquila and Priscilla travel with Paul to Ephesus, AD 54.*
- *The couple, already present in Rome, receive greetings from Paul (after Claudius died in late AD 54), AD 56.*

---

1. Information collected from Acts 20:4, Eph 6:21, 2 Tim 4:12, Acts 19:29, 2 Tim 4:19, and 1 Cor 16:17.

THE PEOPLE PAUL ADMIRED

- *The couple, living again in Ephesus, send greetings in Paul's letter to Corinth, AD 57.*
- *Paul sends greetings to them in a letter to Timothy, currently in Asia, presumably Ephesus, perhaps AD 64.*

It would have been fun to interview Prisca (her formal name; Priscilla was a name close friends used) and Aquila (Latin for eagle) about their house church initiatives. Can we make an informed guess as to some of their answers if Tychicus—sent by Paul with letters for Ephesus, Colossae, and Philemon—wrote a report? When Tychicus passed through Ephesus with Onesimus, Prisca and Aquila were possibly again resident there after starting a church in Rome.

If you will use this to speak to a group, some members could take the parts of Aquila, Prisca, and Tychicus.

ROUND 1: PEOPLE IN CONTEXT

I am Tychicus. Our ship landed at Ephesus this morning, and we walked up the eleven-meter-wide, stone-paved Harbor Street with shops on either side. This is my first visit to Ephesus, and we will visit big-name leaders Prisca and Aquila, so I shall write about them for you and tell their views about church, too. I shall put in my questions and observations as well.

People crowded up and down Harbor Street, donkey trains carried loads, men plodded past with backloads of goods for the port, merchants hawked their wares, and children guided flocks of sheep through to the hills. It lived up to all one expects of the main city of the busy province of Asia, with its traders, industrious economy, and splendid buildings.

The huge theater sits on the slope of Mount Prion. We passed the gymnasium where actors train, the baths, the Prytaneion temple with altars and sacred fire for the god, and then the tall and impressive pillar-fronted library. More buildings stand along the way: the palace of the proconsul and the basilica for commercial transactions that supplement the wide agora where haggling and business deals take place.

The terraced houses on the right on the way up the paved road will be the place to look for Prisca and Aquila. These are upper-class accommodations near the Tyrannus lecture hall, where I hear Paul, too, taught the good news. I ask directions until I reach their doorway. I slip off my sandals and accept the invitation to enter. The house is handsome, with frescoes on the walls and the floors paved with mosaic. Perhaps they keep a house in the city and walk out daily to their tent-making workshop outside the city.

Here come the two people I want to meet. Aquila wears a long, belted Jewish robe, but has his hair short in the Roman style and no beard. Prisca looks the upper-class Greek woman in her woolen tunic and a long cloak with red madder-dyed border for her wrap. Her hair forms a pile on her head.

"Grace and peace, Aquila and Prisca. I'm pleased to meet you. I have a letter from Brother Paul for the believers in Ephesus."

Aquila: That's wonderful. Welcome, welcome. We're so pleased to meet you, too.

Myself: Meet my companion Onesimus. We are on our way up the valley to Colossae.

Prisca: You, too, are welcome, Onesimus. Come in, both, and have a late breakfast with us. I hope your sea journey went well.

Myself: Yes, though it is always a relief to make land and be away from the risk of storms and pirates.

Aquila: True. But robbers and riots provide too much excitement on land, as I'm sure you know.

Myself: You're right. I suppose robbers affect your tent-making business, too.

Aquila: I usually work with a household, and that can include a guard at the workshop. Right from when we arrived here, we have kept an open home for people who come to us personally. Did you hear how Apollos became one of our first guests in Ephesus?

Myself: I certainly did. He's a highly regarded teacher these days. I heard him in Corinth. He tells how you brought him to your place, made him feel at home, and together taught him how God entered the world in the person of Christ. Now, he shows how the documents of the old law point to Jesus as the Messiah. Excellent linguist and a great way with words. You can be proud of him. You as a couple must have learned several languages, too.

Prisca: Yes, that's true. We came originally from Pontus,[2] so we worked in a local language as well as Hebrew and the Greek that reaches across borders. In Rome, we needed Latin; in Corinth, we needed both

---

2. Mountainous Pontus is on the Turkish coast of the Black Sea.

classical and common Greek; and here, there are local dialects, too. We're adaptable now, but it's hard work for our visitors sometimes.

Myself: You are much more educated than most women, Prisca.

Prisca: Yes, it's from my educated family, but I keep working on languages to spread the message about Christ.

Myself: Coming from a highborn position like that, how did you both learn a trade?

Aquila: It's a Jewish custom. I started my apprenticeship when I was thirteen, and Priscilla picked up tent-making skills too. It's a longstanding trade. Think how Abraham and Isaac lived in tents. They are still an important commodity. These days, we have to be smart on the business side too—quality materials, employee management, sales. Having a trade is also a policy for us. We believe it is right to earn our way.

Prisca: It's helpful when we have a business partner, too, as when Paul stayed with us in Corinth. Rabbis commonly support themselves without asking payment for teaching. By working with our enterprise, Paul did not have to cover the outlay on new materials when he was not a permanent resident.

Myself: Tell me what you do as a tentmaker.

Prisca: We make all kinds of tents, canopies, and awnings, both leather and woven. The military outfitters buy many tents, and street-stall holders purchase awnings.

Aquila: We procure tanned leather, and our task is to cut it to the right dimensions, then to shape and stitch it together with awls of various sizes. Our instruments are easily carried, allowing us to move from place to place.

Myself: I notice some tents are woven. How does that work?

Prisca: For those, we purchase woven lengths of black goat-hair cloth, often from Cilicia, the area where our friend Paul grew up. It is porous, but shrinks and becomes waterproof the first time it gets wet. We and our employees stitch it to tent design and add ropes and loops along with side curtains made of the goat-hair cloth or of reed matting.

Aquila: The business means we have a large household and many opportunities to tell visitors about Jesus. Paul asked us to come from Corinth to Ephesus specifically to set up house because he saw what we were doing and wanted it taken further. Then, he encouraged us to do the same in Rome, and now we are back here, again with a church in our home.

The Couple Ministry of Priscilla and Aquila in Ephesus

Myself: I hear Paul worked with you in the business in Corinth and here.

Prisca: Yes, those two years brought a new experience for us, too. Paul wore an apron while he worked and often a kerchief around his brow as well. People asked if they could borrow his kerchief or apron and lay them on sick people, and, surprisingly, they were healed. For a while, Paul hired a hall here in Ephesus to give more teaching. Our service is different. We focus on gatherings in our home. We'll get a room ready for you now. Please stay long enough to join us on Sunday evening.

Myself: Thank you. I certainly shall.

ROUND 2: MEETING IN PROGRESS

I have explored the city and found out more about Ephesus with its nearly 200,000 people. It has a fine harbor at the mouth of the river Cayster. Having developed at the end of the caravan route from Syria through Anatolia to Asia, it thrums with shipping from Greece, Rome, and other ports. This city lights up Asia as an outpost of Greek and Roman arts. It also focuses for Asia the hugely popular religion of the goddess Artemis (often called Diana) that superimposes itself on the old spells, magic, demons, gods, and exorcists.

I walked up the rise to see the temple of Artemis, where thousands come on pilgrimage and buy silver miniatures of part of the temple and goddess to wear as charms. It is magnificent: 425 feet long and 220 feet wide with 117 huge stone columns. People call it one of the Seven Wonders of the World. Artemis is the goddess of forests and hunting, the embodiment of fertility, the patron of maidens of marriageable age, and the helper of women in childbirth. Her temple is fabulously wealthy and surrounded with woods, gardens, dining rooms, picnic sites, and marriage halls. I can see why Paul wanted the top church-founding team of Prisca and Aquila here. It is such a center of religion.

As people were arriving, I asked Aquila and Prisca to tell me more about the church in their house. (There is at least one other church here, in the home of Onesiphorus.) They have made such a specialty out of using their home that they can explain the theory behind it as well as the practice.

Aquila: Hospitality lives out the very nature of the gospel. God is like a welcoming host, serving people, sharing the table for communion

THE PEOPLE PAUL ADMIRED

bread and wine. Such a welcome unites people, leaving aside the barriers in society of race, pure and impure, and status levels.

Prisca: I still find it exciting to see all the variety and think about the breakdown of differences. Those between rich and poor broke down early, back in Jerusalem right after Pentecost. The barriers between conservative Christ-believing Jews in Palestine and Greek-speaking believing Jews from all around the Mediterranean Sea required work, such as setting up deacons to ensure fairness. That has become less an issue. Ritual cleanness or uncleanness along the lines of Jew and non-Jew took much longer. Believers now eat together and share a common communion cup. I believe we have come a long way here.

Myself: This gathering already looks remarkable, with so many different people in your home.

Aquila: Come and let me point out some of our people. These are Cleo and Avis. You probably noticed their Roman-style togas. Cleo is an engineer helping design the new buildings the city is putting up. Sitting next to them is Gordio, a sailor off one of the boats. His native language is Luvian, as he comes from Troy, but he now speaks some Greek, too. Here comes one of our helpers, Cybele, bringing lamb broth for Gershon and his wife Zahava. Gershon sells incense that he imports from Jerusalem. He's originally a Jerusalem merchant.

Myself, wondering under my breath: Gershon and Zahava are Jewish names. Cybele is not a Jewish name, and yet she's cooking and serving for everyone. Lamb broth! And Aquila does not even stop to say if it is kosher or not! This couple has obviously stopped thinking about customary purity, just as Paul wanted.

Prisca: You would only see this in a gathering of Christ-followers, don't you think? See the two young women across the room with their hair drawn back with combs? Elena and Sophronia grew up here in Ephesus. Their father's Greek, Myron. He works in the city library. See him talking to the three Asian fishermen over there? On the left, you can see Katazuli and Lubarnas, who came on pilgrimage from Galatia to worship at the Artemis temple. At an inn, they met the older couple by the wall on the right, who taught them about Christ.

Do you see the couple seated on the rush mats? They are from Cenchrea and talking to two new people who were brought as slaves from Crete. Aphrodisia is doing well in learning Greek in the household where she works. We are saving toward buying freedom for them.

The Couple Ministry of Priscilla and Aquila in Ephesus

Myself: I heard about this, Prisca, but still it is remarkable. Your friends eat and talk together in a private home. The barriers between Jews and non-Jews and other races are simply not there, nor are the barriers between upper class and lower class, free or slave. All are friends. I saw this in the churches in Rome, too, but I think you did it here sooner.

Aquila: As you may imagine, it makes us so warm inside as we look around.

Myself, still wondering under my breath: I can see some small children, but not many. That must be the same as in many other places. Sad how many children die in their first year and how many more before they reach age six.

The children's chatter quiets as the people sing a song led by someone with a strong voice and a hand drum. Several pray to God, but, of course, there is no visible god to worship. Now, look at this. All take the communion symbols, bread shared and a cup passed around. I still think this is astounding. The Jewish separatism and barriers are quite simply not here.

Prisca brings the rolled parchment. The special feature this evening is the letter from Paul that I have brought. We listen as Aquila reads and realize that part of what Paul describes is exactly what we have seen. Paul knew how the church in the home of Prisca and Aquila functioned and wrote of it.

Aquila, reading: "Remember that formerly you who are Gentiles by birth and called 'uncircumcised.' . . . But now, in Christ Jesus, you who once were far away have been brought near through the blood of Christ. For he himself is our peace, who has made the two one and has destroyed the barrier, the dividing wall of hostility, by abolishing in his flesh the law with its commandments and regulations. His purpose was to create in himself one new humanity out of the two, thus making peace. . . . Consequently, you are no longer foreigners and aliens, but fellow citizens with God's people and members of God's household."

Myself, still thinking: I love the blessing I receive when I come to a believers' gathering. In my old life, I would never have thought such a thing possible. This is the shape of Christian fellowship. This is what hosts and hostesses are achieving, and it requires both, men like Aquila and women like Prisca, when there is a couple. This could not be pushed by men on women. Women are often more conservative, and conservative

THE PEOPLE PAUL ADMIRED

people do not inter-dine, welcome outsiders, or pray together. Yet, this is what is happening.

ROUND 3: TURBULENT TIMES

Myself: Thank you, indeed, for inviting me to stay these few nights. Can I take some of your time this morning? I want to write a little more. Do tell me about the dangers you have faced because of your house church.

Aquila: Yes, it's been a bumpy road at times—bumpier than the noisy chariot over the big stones out there this morning. The city's so large that, when Paul came back, he came upon people we had not met: disciples who needed to know about the Holy Spirit. He taught them, of course. He lectured for two years and healed people. Then occurred the much-talked-about incident when one of the seven sons of the Jew Sceva tried to cast out a demon in the name of Jesus, and it leapt on some of them and injured them.

Not only were Jews attracted to our message, but so many Greeks gave allegiance to Jesus that sales of the silver Artemis shrine models fell drastically, and people held a public bonfire of their books of magic and spells—items worth 50,000 drachmas. The city merchants of Artemis icons were extremely upset about that, as you can imagine. That led to a riot, stirred on by Demetrius, one of the silversmiths whose business was suffering.

Think of the honor and shame issues. Society does not see people as individuals, but always as part of a group, and what an individual does reflects on the whole group. Demetrius easily convinced people, especially the silversmiths, that, if the silver shrines did not sell, not only would they have less income, but their guild, their god, and their city would suffer shame. No wonder they shouted and rioted. It made life exceedingly dangerous for us. The town clerk needed all his skill to quiet that one.

Prisca: Yes, we lived at risk along with Brother Paul and the other believers. We could have lost our lives. We persuaded Paul not to speak in front of the crowd in the big open-air theater. Paul knows we have risked our lives for him and the others. It goes with the territory. We would do it again. We are not going to let fear stop us telling about Jesus. But we do not have to ask for trouble. I have certainly been terrified at times. Some disciples have suffered and given their lives. It could happen to us one day. God does not make us immune to suffering.

The Couple Ministry of Priscilla and Aquila in Ephesus

Aquila: Suffering is something we as a couple talk through together. We have to be fully agreed and let the Holy Spirit come through in our thoughts and feelings. If one bemoaned the other's risk-taking, or if one wanted to pull back and hide behind our business and avoid trouble, disunity would quickly undermine our strength as a couple and our ministry vision. We are partners in trade, travel, home, hospitality, and teaching.

Myself: I think I spot another angle that boosts your effectiveness. You spent time in the company of experienced Paul to learn, and then you spent time in the company of less-experienced ministers, like Apollos, to pass on what you know. That must be a pattern to look to as well.

Prisca: Now that you point out those two examples, yes. They came prior to thinking about a pattern, but that is what we teach: Learn from people who went before you and pass it on.

Myself: I have another question for your, Prisca. Look how often you have shifted from place to place. Does it never worry you to set up and dismantle your home so often?

Prisca: You haven't known me long, Tychicus, or you would not need to ask. We love the homemaking in order to be hospitable and provide for people, but it is a means to an end, not an end in itself. I guess you would call us people-focused. We reach out for the sake of Jesus Christ and for the sake of people. Growing churches is our passion, and we happily shift house to do it. Think how we have friends all around the world now: Corinth, Rome, here. It's because of one major thing—a church that meets in our home.

READER REFLECTION

When you finish reading the chapter on Priscilla and Aquila, pause to reflect on how you came to have a house or apartment or room to live in, and thank God for it. Consider ways in which your home is and can be an instrument to serve others and serve Christ.

SPEAKER/LISTENER EXPLORATION

If you used the chapter on Aquila and Priscilla to speak to a group, make two lists with the group: aspects of a house church that applied only to Ephesus in the first century, and aspects of a house church that apply today. What can you learn from these?

12

Paul Teaches in Rome

Welcome to a Rented House

SCRIPTURE SOURCES: Acts 28:17–31, Romans 16, 2 Timothy 4:21, Titus 3:12, Philemon

KNOWN HOUSEHOLD CHRIST-GATHERINGS IN ROME IN HOMES OF: Paul, Priscilla and Aquila, Aristobulus, Narcissus

GROUPS WHO WERE TOGETHER IN SOME WAY, PERHAPS HOUSEHOLD CHRIST-GATHERINGS:

GROUP 1: Asyncritus, Phlegon, Hermes, Patrobas, Hermas

GROUP 2: Philologus, Julia, Nereus, the sister of Nereus, Olympas

GROUP 3: people in household service of the Caesar (Phil 4:22)

GROUP 4: people sending greetings: Eubulus, Pudens, Linus, Claudia (2 Tim 4:21)

HIGHLY RECOMMENDED CHRISTIAN WORKERS:

WOMEN: Mary, Junia, Tryphena, Tryphosa, Persis, the mother of Rufus

MEN: Andronicus, Urbanus, Apelles, Rufus

PAUL'S FURTHER ACQUAINTANCES AND HELPERS IN ROME: Ampliatus, Stachys, Herodion, Artemis, Tychicus, Epaphras, Mark, Aristarchus, Demas, Luke, Onesimus, Timothy

Paul Teaches in Rome

*C*HRISTIANS TODAY KNOW PAUL *for his theology and missionary zeal. For this chapter, however, the focus must on be Paul as a house church leader. Can we see him as friend and host? Perhaps the mother of Rufus could describe Paul's arrival and hospitality in Rome, if she were educated and had access to his writing.*

Paul—what a dear friend he has become to Rufus and to me. Open to everyone. We had met earlier, but it took me a long time to realize how he must have changed after that vision on the road to Damascus. My son Rufus and I are used to Latin ways, having lived here all our lives, although we are Jews. When I first mentioned Paul to a Pharisee acquaintance, Eliakim, we noticed his angry reaction. We were discussing a business deal at a shop run by a Jewish man who serves fish, bread, and leafy vegetables. It was kosher, but Eliakim would not eat with us.

"Have you heard that Saul of Tarsus, now called Paul, is on his way to Rome?" Eliakim asked.

"Yes, friends say he is under arrest," I explained. "He is chained to a soldier, and with him are Luke and Aristarchus. They made new friends in Puteoli and now have the forty-three miles to walk to here."

"I guess you heard he's a Pharisee, but now he even eats with Gentiles—and eats nonkosher food." Rufus turned to Eliakim.

"Pah! I've heard no good of that renegade!" Eliakim snarled. "I don't believe he is genuine. No Pharisee would do that. A real Pharisee never, ever eats nonkosher food. He is a scoundrel and a traitor to God in Heaven."

"You sound very angry."

"I am angry. Pharisees serve and fear God. They have a passion for purity for God. They avoid contact with pagans, and even fellow Jews. Fellow Jews are *Amharez,* unclean. Only Pharisees are clean. In Jerusalem, I would not even talk to you. We worked to get rid of that Jesus of Nazareth because he associated with ordinary people. They are sinners."

"But surely Jesus was a good man!"

"Pshah! Good? He ate without washing his hands or his cup. He touched a dead child. He let a woman touch his cloak in public. He touched blind men who were cursed by God. This Saul is no better. I'll tell him what I think of him if I get a chance!"

We knew where Eliakim's thinking came from, but his vehemence surprised us. We had become accustomed to more open views. The conversation dwindled and finished. Rufus and I left the next day to hike,

THE PEOPLE PAUL ADMIRED

with some of our acquaintances, the two days' journey to meet our friend Paul and his friends at The Three Taverns to the south. It was a treat to meet him again, and he kissed us all and remembered all our names. Captain Julius let him walk with just one foot-soldier to whose arm Paul was chained. Paul was almost overwhelmed that so many of us came to meet him.

"Thank you, thank you so much," he exclaimed. "I'm thrilled you have all come. I've learned to love so much the people who follow Jesus the Messiah." He seemed to gain courage from seeing us. We all walked, talking, as we covered the remaining thirty-five miles back along the Appian Way. Paul wasted no time after his arrival. He offered to meet the leaders of the 40,000 Jews of Rome within three days because he wanted to explain himself.

"My brothers," he said, "I was arrested in Jerusalem more than two years ago when people thought I took a Greek into the temple. I did not do such a thing. I have not done anything against our temple or our people. The Romans would have released me, because I did not deserve the death penalty, but the Jews objected, so I had to appeal to Caesar. I did not want to charge my own people with a crime. That is why I asked to see you now that I am here. I am under arrest because I speak of our God and our hope as the people of Israel."

"Nobody sent us any letters about you," the leaders reported. "We haven't heard much about you. But we want to hear your views, for we know people everywhere are talking against this sect." They set up a meeting to hear more another day, and even more of the curious came to the place where Paul was staying, including our acquaintance Eliakim. That was a long day. Paul talked from morning until evening, appealing to the five books of the law of Moses and many of the prophecies, trying to persuade them that Jesus was the anointed Messiah.

"I believe everything in the Law and Prophets, but I worship the God of our fathers as a follower of the Way," he stated. "I hope for the resurrection of the dead, both the righteous and the wicked. As a young man, I conformed to the strictest codes of the Pharisees and tried to get rid of anybody who taught otherwise, especially people who believed in Jesus." He then told how God spoke to him in a spectacular way on the road to Damascus. That sure brought discussion and disagreement among them.

"How impossible for a man who died on a cross to be the Messiah," said some.

Paul Teaches in Rome

"Such a person is cursed, not a savior," Eliakim snorted.

"But think how he teaches people to love. The teaching of Jesus is so different. The argument comes from higher moral ground," claimed others.

Paul knew his message would split their loyalties. Some followed his teaching, and some rejected it outright. He was ready for that, too, and told them that if they did not want God's gift, he would offer it to the Gentiles. At that, most left, but a few of these Roman Jews asked to come back.

"Yes, do," Paul invited. "We are planning to rent a house."

Paul asked me then to give some housekeeping and hospitality advice to Rufus and Luke, and they soon had the furniture and kitchen set up.

What did people notice when they attended Paul's teaching sessions by the light from a torch flame on a stick or an olive oil lamp in his rented home? There was no priest. Paul was a teacher who shared ceremonies like the memory supper with others. He did not baptize anyone in the Tiber, either, since he was confined to the house. He gave opportunities to the young men he was mentoring, letting them teach and serve. For the weekly service, there were prayer, singing, old law reading and gospel reading, prophecy, interpretation, and Paul's teaching. Paul had helped so many people start and run a church, and now, at last, late in his life, circumstances forced him to stay in one place, so he ran a church himself. Roman believers grew in number, including some people from Caesar's household.

Herodion, Aristobulus, and a few others of Jewish background reached the house one afternoon to ask Paul more questions and seek more teaching. Instead of lounging on the couches, guests sat upright to fit more people in the room.

Herodion asked the first questions. "You were a Pharisee, Paul. What changed you so much?"

"I assure you it was a huge learning curve," Paul replied. "I and my crowd hemmed ourselves in with so many rules we could not see that our thinking was unjust. Jesus said, 'Woe to you, teachers of the law and Pharisees, you hypocrites! You give a tenth of your spices—mint, dill, and cumin. But you have neglected the weightier matters of the law: *justice, mercy, and faithfulness*.' We sure failed. We focused on little rules and missed out on mercy and justice."

THE PEOPLE PAUL ADMIRED

"Then what about levels of society, Paul?" Aristobulus queried from another couch. "Pharisees think themselves above everyone else."

"That was a shock to me, Aristobulus. The very people we Pharisees despised, the supposedly 'lower' levels, were the ones Jesus spent his time with. He happily welcomed them to join the kingdom. He told these despised people the wonderful welcoming parables of the lost sheep, the lost coin, and the lost son. I had lived and practiced our religious, class, and cultural pride. I agreed with them that other Jews 'know nothing of the law. There is a curse on them.' When I heard how Jesus loved them, I was ashamed. I had thought I was so great. I hung my head. I had to learn that God loves all people equally. Nobody is a nobody. That sure took me a while to work out."

The Jews on the couches were sitting bolt upright now. They had never in all their lives heard of a Pharisee who hung his head or thought nobody was a nobody. Pharisees are so sharp and educated.

"Then what about your great ability as a debater, scoring points off people? You seem to love people now," hazarded Aristobulus. "Pharisees choose their leaders by scholarly achievement and believe debating and disagreeing over the meaning of the Torah imitates God. I hear you used to win all those debates."

"Yes. It won me position there. I pompously approved when the Jews killed Stephen. He had transgressed their system. I stood arrogantly, full of myself. We were *right*. Everybody else was *wrong*. Jesus had to crush my pride."

I had a comment here: "Paul, what you say about the Pharisees makes me shudder. I can hardly believe you ever belonged with them. Your teaching and actions on class and race were so exclusivist."

"Yes, it's true. I was a dominating, hard-hitting stickler for rules."

"I can only say I'm glad you changed, Paul," I sighed. "You love and respect Rufus and me, even me as a woman. You heal sick people, race does not matter to you, and you eat with anybody."

"I can vouch for that, too," Timothy commented, coming with clay cups of water for the guests. "Paul makes friends wherever he goes. Even with Captain Julius, who ordered the guards not to kill him when the ship grounded on Malta. Even with the elderly official on the island, Publius, who gave generous hospitality."

Timothy and Luke went out shortly for firewood and supplies from the market. Paul, the welcoming host, plied the guests with snacks of

Paul Teaches in Rome

raisins and walnuts. As the day lengthened, he lit the oil lamps and found an extra cushion for an elderly guest.

He does it like an experienced host, I thought. One would not guess he had roamed the world on foot and on horseback for the last twenty years or more, never with his own home. He is the visible model of a considerate gentleman. Indeed, he had more than a score of friends in Rome before he arrived. Now he has many more. I'm old enough to be his mother, but sometimes I think Paul acts with the warmth of a mother, even though, when he was a Pharisee, he was extreme in hardness, control, and the use of force. We are still enjoying the contrast. I'll ask for more details.

"Paul, this is such an amazing transformation. Tell us more," I said aloud.

"I deluded myself." Paul leaned back on the couch. "I was paranoid about rules, especially on purity. I kept hundreds of rules for washing, eating, tithing, and not touching women, or Amharez, or Gentiles, or sick people, or people with leprosy, or the body of a dead person. Jesus did not worry about all that. He taught love. I was stunned when I realized that. Jesus showed that we Pharisees were hypocrites: 'Everything they do is done for people to see: They love the place of honor at banquets and the most important seats in the synagogues; they love to be greeted with respect in the marketplaces and to have people call them Rabbi.' Jesus taught, 'You are not to be called 'Rabbi,' for you have only one Master *and you are all brothers.* . . . The greatest among you will be your *servant!*' That ran contrary to all I ever lived and studied as a Pharisee.

"I heard that Jesus reprimanded us, 'Woe to you, teachers of the law and Pharisees, you hypocrites! You travel over land and sea to win a single convert and then make that convert twice as much a child of hell as you are. . . . Woe to you, blind guides! . . . On the outside you appear to people as righteous, but on the inside you are full of hypocrisy and wickedness.' I cringed. This pungent rebuke was about me."

"How did you learn love instead of rules, Paul?" my son Rufus asked.

"How could I not? Jesus loved even those who shouted 'Crucify him!' He prayed, 'Jerusalem, Jerusalem, you who kill the prophets and stone those sent to you, how often I have longed to gather your children together as a hen gathers her chicks under her wings, and you were not willing.'"

THE PEOPLE PAUL ADMIRED

Paul arranged regular teaching afternoons that soon crowded his rented house. One afternoon, as a winter wind cooled the air, several Latin speakers chatted with Paul. Urbanus asked what faith meant to Paul. He smiled when he heard Paul rattle off at speed all the things he used to trust in.

"If others think they have reasons to put confidence in the flesh, I have more: circumcised on the eighth day, of the people of Israel, of the tribe of Benjamin, a Hebrew of the Hebrews; in regard to the law, a Pharisee, as for zeal, persecuting the church; as for righteousness based on the law, faultless."

"Is that all?" laughed Julia.

"No, there's more," he grinned. "I can boast with any fool. Are they Hebrews? So am I. Are they Israelites? So am I. Are they Abraham's descendants? So am I. Are they servants of Christ? (I am out of my mind to talk like this.) I am more."

"You certainly changed," Urbanus chuckled. "It's mind-blowing. I have heard you now champion women, Gentiles, and people with disabilities. You don't care whether a person is slave, free, or freedman, do you? You love the jailor and the people in the jail!"

"Yes, I wrote in one of my letters, 'Though I am free and belong to no one, I have made myself a slave to everyone to win as many as possible.'"

"You teach the same in the mission teams, too," Julia noted. "You are not the founder-manager of teams or supervisor of new churches. You hand over control. You think each team is capable of running a church to fit their own circumstances. You begin letters by praising friends all over the empire. You trust them for their tasks and honor them for their work."

"I notice your instructions to husbands and wives, too," Urbanus went on. "You tell them both to love the other with sacrificial love and both to submit to the other."

"How else could they act, Urbanus? It can never be real friendship if one is the boss. I aim to keep deep personal friendships with both men and women, respect their achievements, expect them both to handle responsibility, and recommend them as a team to others."

I noticed that perspective in action when Paul wrote to us in Rome before he came in person. He greeted nine women friends and evangelists along with nineteen men. He urged all believers to preach or prophesy and expected women to be part of that. Paul also expected both women and men to make responsible decisions in marriage. He is so balanced. He

Paul Teaches in Rome

wrote, "The wife does not have authority over her own body, but yields it to her husband. In the same way, the husband does not have authority over his own body, but yields it to his wife."[1] He told wives to love husbands with the sacrificial love that fits around the other's needs, and he told husbands to love wives with sacrificial love that is unconditional. The instruction is the same. Jewish literature often says the same thing in two different ways.[2]

Julia and I sometimes felt warm inside when Paul said he was like a mother to the women and men he knew in the churches. He told the Corinthians they were immature, needing mother's milk. When the unmarried Paul spoke like this, you can see how comfortably he affirmed women in the churches.

He acted similarly with other cultures. He respected them, such as when he addressed the Greeks at the Areopagus in Athens. He wrote at length on reconciliation of Jews and Gentiles. He saw them as former strangers now joined to make a temple. Paul cared about disabled and ill people, too. Luke told us how in Lystra a congenitally lame man sat listening to Paul. When Paul realized he had faith and told him to stand up, the man jumped up and walked. Paul healed people in Ephesus, raised Eutychus when he fell from the window, and healed the father of Publius and then other people on Malta.

Something remarkable was happening at Paul's rented house. People crowded there through the congested city lanes. They passed religious processions and sacrifices, festival arrays and weddings, funerals, masquerades, graffiti, and edicts on the walls. Life is lived in the streets. Scribes and tinkers fill the recesses, town criers and soapbox orators the corners. Dogs lick up the garbage. Hawkers push their carts. A Latin writer commented cynically that there was noise all night, carts creaking through narrow winding streets and the curses of drivers caught in the traffic. He said rented houses were squalid, noisy, expensive, and cold, with no running water and no toilet. At the same time, Nero's government was floundering and plots against him increased. The salaries of his soldiers were in arrears, and he gave their wellbeing little attention.

---

1. 1 Cor 7:4.

2. *Hupotassomai, agapaō*, Eph 5:22, 25. Some people believe Paul taught that husbands must control wives. Such teaching would make Paul a hypocrite, preaching one thing and practising another, for in practice he recognised women as decision makers along with their husbands (See 1 Cor 7).

THE PEOPLE PAUL ADMIRED

Out of this heaving urban melee, Paul's guests pass through the door to a haven of welcome. He is such a kindly man! Yes, he carefully teaches correct theology, holy living, and evangelism. Yes, he is focused on the teaching he wants to give the people in front of him, but even before he reached Rome, we knew this was only one side of him. We are also genuinely his dear friends. Humbly and lovingly, he places himself alongside others as a team player accountable to the group. Let me tell you some things I observed. Paul praised many people to their faces and expressed admiration for them to others. He honored the work of Prisca and Aquila. He praised former slave Onesimus. He reconciled with John Mark and honored him in spite of an earlier difference. He saw Timothy and Titus as his own sons in the faith. He called us in Rome dear friends, outstanding, hard workers, trustworthy, hospitable. He saw me like a mother. People loved Paul in Troas, Ephesus, Caesarea, Tyre, Ptolemais, and many other places.

This was not shallow lack of discernment. I know he grieved for his fellow Jews. He wrote concerning them, "I have great sorrow and unceasing anguish in my heart. For I could wish that I myself were cursed and cut off from Christ for the sake of my people." Luke told us that, when his Ephesus friends of different race, class, culture, and former creed bid him farewell, he wept as they embraced him and kissed him. Then he knelt down with all of them and prayed. From an angry, self-righteous persecutor, he has become a loving, kind encourager.

While the emperor grows increasingly unpopular, Paul's court case has dragged on without a hearing. We think there may be a backlog of cases, or they are waiting for the prosecution to present a case, but it may be that hearing the case does not suit the emperor's convenience. In the meantime, Paul hardly sees the smart side of Rome: the marble temples, fountains, statues, the palace of the Caesar, the seven hills, or even the Tiber River. He cannot attend theaters, public baths, or chariot races on the Circus Maximus. He hardly sees the city's conspicuous consumption with wealthy wives in fancy clothes and the clamor for honor by the wealthy inscribing their names on public works—but, perhaps, that is just as well. He would be distressed by the decadence.

Sometimes, Paul experiences the comfort of his own countrymen around him. Helpers at times include Mark, Jesus called Justus, Tychicus, Onesimus, Demas, Luke, Timothy, Crescens (until he left recently for Dalmatia, as did Titus). At different stages, Aristarchus and Epaphras have been imprisoned with Paul. Still, he faces the ups and downs of human relations as people come and go. At his first defense, when no one came to his support, Paul admitted to us that he felt humanly deserted, but he was still strengthened as he felt the Lord standing by his side. He always feels warmed by receiving and sending letters, and he continues to enjoy sending greetings from friend to friend.

Because God has changed Paul's heart, turning him from a difficult, demanding Pharisee to a loving friend, Paul now experiences for himself the joy of sharing in a growing, learning, loving fellowship in his own home. The method he and many others designed is now at work in the capital of the empire. I know it will succeed in time, bringing the gospel to the full diversity of the city in education, gender, race, religion, caste, and class. I am so blessed to be a small part of the great mission.

READER REFLECTION

When you finish reading the chapter on Paul, praise God for the way such a man changed. Examine your own life for spiritual growth, and pray for areas you want to change more, especially in relating with warmth and respect to greatly diverse people.

SPEAKER/LISTENER EXPLORATION

If you used the chapter on Paul to speak to a group, ask them to construct a list, with examples, of ways in which Paul changed as he moved from Pharisee to apostle and finally to house church leader. Then, pause to consider ways God has helped group members change in their own lives.

Bibliography

Banks, Robert. *Going to Church in the First Century.* NSW, Australia: Hexagon Press, 1980, 1985.

———. *Paul's Idea of Community.* Peabody, MA: Hendrickson, 1994.

Bilezikian, Gilbert. *Beyond Sex Roles.* Grand Rapids: Baker, 1985.

Bruce, F. F. *The Pauline Circle.* Flemington Markets: Paternoster, 1985.

Cahill, Lisa Sowle. *Family: A Christian Social Perspective.* Minneapolis: Fortress, 2000.

Capper, Brian. "Public Body, Private Women: The Ideology of Gender and Space and the Exclusion of Women from Public Leadership in the Late First Century Church." In *Theology and the Body*, edited by Robert Hannaford and J'annine Jobling, Pp. 123–51. Leominster, UK: Gracewing, 1999.

Cohick, Lyn. *Women in the World of the Earliest Christians: Illuminating Ancient Ways of Life.* Grand Rapids: Baker, 2009.

Duduit, Michael. "Expository Preaching in a Narrative World: An Interview with Haddon Robinson." *Preaching*, n.d. http://www.preaching.com/resources/articles/11565763/.

Editors of Reader's Digest. *After Jesus: The Triumph of Christianity.* New York: Reader's Digest, 1992.

Elwell, Walter, editor. *Evangelical Commentary on the Bible.* Grand Rapids: Baker, 1994.

Evans, Craig, and Stanley Porter, editors. *Dictionary of New Testament Background.* Downers Grove: InterVarsity, 2000.

Fleming, Dean. *Contextualization in the New Testament.* Leicester: InterVarsity, 2005.

Freeman, James. *Manners and Customs of the Bible.* Plainfield, NJ: Logos, 1972.

Giles, Kevin. *Patterns of Ministry among the First Christians.* New York: Harper-Collins, 1989.

Green, Michael. *Evangelism in the Early Church.* Grand Rapids: Eerdmans, 1970.

Greenleaf, Robert. *Servant Leadership.* New York: Paulist, 1977.

Hawthorne, Gerald, Ralph P. Martin, and Daniel G. Reid, editors. *Dictionary of Paul and his Letters.* Downers Grove: InterVarsity, 1993.

Hellerman, Joseph. *The Ancient Church as Family.* Minneapolis: Fortress, 2001.

Jeffers, James S. *The Greco-Roman World of the New Testament Period.* Downers Grove: InterVarsity, 1999.

Keener, Craig. *The IVP Bible Background Commentary, New Testament.* Downers Grove: InterVarsity, 1993.

Kroeger, Catherine Clark, and Mary Evans, editors. *The IVP Women's Bible Commentary.* Downers Grove: InterVarsity, 2002.

Bibliography

Luter, Boyd. "Partnership in the Gospel: The Role of Women in the Church of Philippi." *Journal of the Evangelical Theological Society* 39, no. 3 (1996): 411–20. http://www.etsjets.org/files/JETS-PDFs/39/39-3/39-3-pp411-420_JETS.pdf.

Luter, Boyd, and Kathy McReynolds. *Women as Christ's Disciples: Models in the New Testament Church.* Geanies House, Ross-shire: Christian Focus, 2003 (reprinted by Baker, 1997).

Malherbe, Abraham. *Social Aspects of Early Christianity.* Philadelphia: Fortress, 1983.

Malina, Bruce J. *The New Testament World: Insights from Cultural Anthropology.* Louisville, KY: Westminster, 1993.

Martin, Ralph P. *James,* Word Biblical Commentary. Waco, TX: Word, 1988.

———. *Worship in the Early Church.* London: Marshall, Morgan, and Scott, 1964.

Martin, Ralph P., and Peter Davids. *Dictionary of the Later New Testament and Its Developments.* Downers Grove: InterVarsity, 1997.

Mickelsen, Alvera. *Did Paul Practice What We're Told He Preached?* Website of Christians for Biblical Equality, http://www.cbeinternational.org/?q=content/did-paul-practice-what-were-told-he-preached, accessed April 25, 2011.

Pfeiffer, Charles, and Howard F. Vos. *The Wycliffe Historical Geography of Bible Lands.* Chicago: Moody, 1967.

Pierce, Ronald, and Rebecca Merrill Groothuis, with Gordon Fee. *Discovering Biblical Equality: Complementary without Hierarchy.* Downers Grove: InterVarsity, 2005.

Rohrbaugh, Richard L. *The Social Sciences and New Testament Interpretation.* Peabody, MA: Hendrickson, 1996.

Sanders, Oswald. *Spiritual Leadership.* Chicago: Moody, 1967.

Schnabel, Eckhard. *Early Christian Mission: Volume 1, Jesus and the Twelve.* Downers Grove: InterVarsity, 2002.

———. *Early Christian Mission: Volume 2, Paul and the Early Church.* Downers Grove: InterVarsity, 2004.

Stalker, James. *Life of Saint Paul.* Edinburgh: T&T Clark, 1885. http://books.google.com/ebooks?id=vToHAAAAQAAJ.

Stambaugh, John E., and David L. Balch. *The New Testament in Its Social Environment.* Philadelphia: Westminster, 1986.

Tenney, Merrill. *New Testament Times.* London: InterVarsity, 1971.

Thompson, J. A. *The Bible and Archaeology,* 3rd edition. Grand Rapids: Eerdmans, 1982.

Tidball, Derek. *An Introduction to the Sociology of the New Testament.* Carlisle, UK: Paternoster, 1983.

Unger, Merrill F. *New Unger's Bible Dictionary,* revised edition. Edited by R. K. Harrison, Howard F. Vos, and Cyril J. Barber. Chicago: Moody, 1988.

Vos, Howard. *Nelson's New Illustrated Bible Manners and Customs.* Nashville, TN: Thomas Nelson, 1999.

Watson, Nigel. "'And if Children, then Heirs' (Rom 8:17)—Why not Sons?" *Australian Biblical Review* 49 (2001): 53–56.

www.ingramcontent.com/pod-product-compliance
Lightning Source LLC
Chambersburg PA
CBHW071502160426
43195CB00013B/2189